MEET MR. OCEAN

The Worst Teacher in the World

Chris Gleason

Meet Mr. Ocean

THE BACKSTORY

This book began as a goofy joke around the house. My daughter Abigail has a really funny teacher with the nickname of Mr. C. I joked that he should have a friend called Mr. Ocean (yeah, I know it doesn't make sense on paper... you kind of have to hear it spoken). The character of a cheap, lazy, and forgetful teacher just came to life kind of quickly, and a set of bedtime stories emerged. I wrote this book because it was a ton of fun to take all of the Mr. Ocean vignettes and try to form them into a broader narrative that made sense and was just as much fun as the bite-sized pieces.

ACKNOWLEDGMENTS

To my wife Michele and my daughter Abigail: thanks for making our home such a fun place. Really. There is more wackiness, more laughing, and more love than I ever knew was possible.

MEET MR. OCEAN

Meet Mr. Ocean

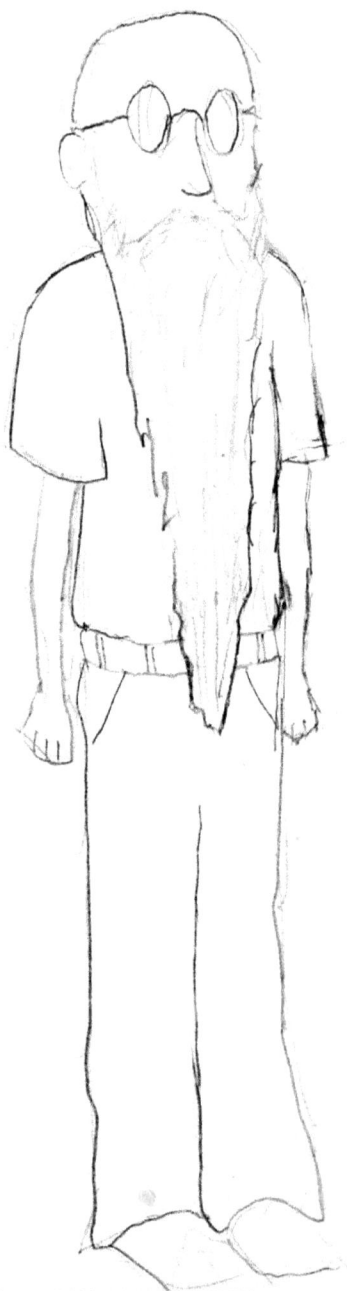

Chapter One

Of course most people are nervous on the first day of school. It's a big change after a summer vacation spent more or less on your own terms, and what's more, there are bound to be plenty of people you don't know yet. So its perfectly natural to be a little anxious. For a particular group of brand new second graders at the Wasatch Arts Academy, however, one terrifying fact stood out above all the others: they had ended up in the classroom of a teacher with quite an unusual reputation. There's no easy way to put this, so I'll just come right out and say it: they had the rotten luck of being in Mr. Ocean's room, and he was widely considered to be the worst teacher in the world. Yes, the world. Not just the city. Not just the state. Not just the country. The. Whole. Entire. World. What exactly made him so lousy? Well, keep reading and you'll find out all about it.

At the beginning of the day, all twenty-one students were feeling pretty freaked out. "What's he really like?" asked a tall boy named Tommy Tibbler in a loud voice. "I heard that he'll chew on your ear lobes if you get a wrong answer!"

"Naw, he isn't that bad," said a girl named Mabel, who had sort of a squeaky voice. "My brother had him a few years ago. I don't think he ever actually hurt anybody. The big thing is that he's just really weird, and really, well, cheap."

The kids puzzled over this. How could a cheapo of a teacher even make a difference? At just that moment, Suzie Longfellow looked at her watch and announced that Mr. Ocean was late. Now this was a first! Since when do teachers show up late? And on the first day, even! Ten minutes later, he finally came in. Strangely, he didn't apologize for being tardy. Weirder still, he didn't seem to realize it.

The next thing the kids noticed was that he was old. I mean super old, like older than anybody you've ever seen before. He was bald, and he had a long, wild beard that went all the way down his chest.

"I bet he could zip that thing into his zipper if he's not careful!" whispered Tommy to a boy named Big Anthony, who was beginning his second year in second grade. And even though he was no stranger to the second grade, it was his first time in Mr. Ocean's room.

He sat at his desk and peered around the room. His glasses were thick, so thick that you could barely even see his eyeballs. After a while he spoke.

"So," he muttered. "It seems to me that you college kids are getting shorter every year. Or maybe I'm getting taller? Nope, that can't be." The kids were just as confused- "Was this guy kidding?" they wondered. Maybe he just had a bad sense of humor.

Finally Mabel raised her hand. "Um, Mr. Ocean? We're not college kids. We're second graders."

"What?" he exclaimed. "I thought I was teaching Math at the University this fall!" He looked deeply troubled at this prospect.

"Uh no, I don't think so," replied Mabel. "I think you've always taught elementary school. In fact, my brother was in your class a few years ago."

"Hmmm," he mused. "What was his name?"

"Rudolf."

"Not Rudolf Finkel? A funny looking kid, with blonde hair that always stuck out in every direction?"

"That's him all right. He's a pain in the butt, but

he's my brother."

Mr. Ocean grimaced. "Rudolf," he groaned. "That kid was a pain in *my* butt too!" The class erupted in laughter- that a teacher let a kid use the word "butt", and then actually said it himself seemed like a pretty good sign.

"Anyway, its all coming back to me now. I've been teaching second grade for about a million years, or at least it seems that way. I guess I was hoping to mix things up a little bit. I asked the principal, Mr. Harvey, last spring if I could have a promotion, and he said yes. I assumed that meant he could get me a job at the University. That would mean a lot more money in my paycheck every week!" The thought of getting a pay raise seemed to fill him with great pleasure, and he even came close to smiling.

"Umm, I think you must be thinking of the old principal," said Annabelle Glazer. "Mr. Harvey retired. We have a new principal now."

"Plus," added Joanna O'Corner, "You can't just get a new job without applying. Did you send in any paperwork?"

"Paperwork, schmaperwork!" he declared dismissively. "And what's this malarkey about a new

Principal? It can't be! Why, the old principal was here for at least forty years! We were old pals! He let me get away with anything!" Immediately his face took on a look of regret. "No, I mean, well, um, he let me, um, become the best teacher I can be." Not a single one of the twenty-one students in the room found this believable. Mr. Ocean was clearly not being entirely honest.

"A new principal?" he complained. "This is the worst news ever!" He was mumbling under his breath, but everybody heard it anyway.

♥   ♥   ♥

A short time later, Mr. Ocean walked back to his supply closet to get some paper. The children looked on curiously and noticed that he appeared to be limping a little bit. It soon became obvious that he had to hold up his pants with one hand as he walked.

"Mr. Ocean," asked Israel Swayze, "Do you need a belt?"

"Ye.!" said Mr. Ocean, "Anybody with eyes in their head can see that I do! But who can afford one

these days? My old one broke in July, and when I went to buy a new one, I couldn't believe it- they cost a fortune! I'm not paying nine dollars for a belt. I've been meaning to go down to the Thrifty Saver; I bet I can get a used one for a dollar."
This was the first time- but not the last- that the kids heard how much their teacher liked the resale store downtown. They would come to learn that it was his second favorite place to shop; his first favorite was the Dollar Store. They imagined that that was because there were never any ugly surprises about how much things cost there.

When he came back to his desk, he took a look at the front of the classroom for what was apparently the first time.

"What the heck is that?" he demanded, pointing at the new smartboard that hung on the wall. "Wait a minute, did we get a big screen tv? Because watching tv is one of my favorite hobbies." His mouth hung open in awe, and he even looked, well, happy.

"Nope, you can't watch tv on it. It's a smartboard," explained Annabelle. "All the classes got them over the summer. They're basically like big tablets. They're hooked up to the internet and you can use them to teach us things."

"Hmph," grunted their teacher. "I'm not convinced. What's wrong with a good old fashioned chalkboard? I don't need any new-fangled teaching tools that have to be plugged in. They'll just end up breaking anyway."

Suzie wondered if that was his real reason for disliking the new technology. Maybe he was just too lazy to learn about it. Or maybe he was just mad that he couldn't watch tv on it.

"Maybe you should just plug it in and try it out," she suggested.

"Plug it in?" he mused. "That's right, it has a power cord, doesn't it?"

"Um, of course it does."

"Suzie, you're a genius!"

"I am?"

"Yup! You gave me a great idea. Tommy, go see if the cord will unplug from that doohickey of a whatchamacallit and bring it over here."

Tommy handed the cord to Mr. Ocean, who quickly threaded it through his belt loops and tied it in a knot at the front of his pants.

"It's a perfect fit!" he exclaimed. "And just think

of the savings!"

This was definitely the strangest thing that any of the kids had ever seen a teacher do. But was it the strangest thing Mr. Ocean would do? Heck no.

Meet Mr. Ocean

Chris Gleason

Chapter Two

As is usually the case on the first day of school, most of the time was spent going over the classroom rules and whatnot. The kids were used to having a daily schedule that let them know what would be happening at any given time, but they didn't see anything like that written out anyplace. This was deeply concerning to most of the kids. Suzie raised her hand and asked about it.

"A schedule? Why do we need a schedule?" Mr. Ocean asked grumpily.

"Um, so we know what we should be studying, and when. Plus, sometimes we'll have to leave the room for other stuff like art and recess and P.E."

Mr. Ocean's face lit up. "Oh, I forgot about that! If you're not here then I can just take a little nap-I mean, um, do some work or something!" Excited by the idea of having some time alone, Mr. Ocean stood up and walked part way to the chalkboard.

"Hmm," he mumbled, "I'm too tired to write on the board. Well, its not so much the writing, but all that standing up seems like a real pain. Who wants to write on the board for me?"

No one raised a hand. Why would they? The kids

were still not sure what to think of Mr. Ocean, and they certainly weren't interested in doing his job for him. In any event, they weren't too impressed just yet.

"Ok then, I'll give out a piece of candy for whoever helps," he announced. This earned a much better response.

Tommy ran to the board and picked up the chalk. All he could find were a few tiny little bits that were just barely big enough to write with. "Don't you have any bigger pieces?" he asked.

"Oh, I used to," said Mr. Ocean matter-of-factly, "But I sold them to the third grade teachers because they were running low."

"Huh?" gulped Mabel. "But that means WE don't have any!"

"True," said Mr. Ocean, "But I got almost four dollars for it. And that reminds me: everybody ask your parents to buy some chalk and send you in with it tomorrow. Parents always expect their kids to need school supplies, so let's not disappoint them."

Suzie shook her head in disbelief. Had her teacher just admitted to selling the chalk for his own

Personal profit? It didn't seem possible. Finally she raised her hand and spoke her mind. "That isn't right, is it? The chalk belongs to all of us!"

You could tell that Mr. Ocean was caught by surprise. "Um, uh," he stammered, "Well, maybe I have plans to spend the four dollars on the class. That would make it ok, wouldn't it?" The kids looked at each other. Maybe it would, most of them thought- but did they trust this guy to actually do it?

"Say, Mr. Ocean?" asked Tommy, who was getting sick of standing around doing nothing at the chalkboard in front of the class. "Shouldn't we be writing down the class schedule?"

"Right, right," said Mr. Ocean, acting as if he'd been meaning to all along. "Now that I think of it, I actually wrote it down on this piece of paper. If you'll just copy it onto the board for me, that'd be great."

Tommy took the paper and groaned. "This looks like a lot of work!" he said. "What if my hand cramps up from all the writing?"

"Just think of that delicious candy- that'll keep you going!"

While Tommy began copying the schedule onto the board, the rest of the class began discussing something else.

"Now," began Mr. Ocean, looking very stern and serious, "There is one last thing we need to cover. Do you all see that door behind me?" He pointed to a regular-looking door that had a small sign on, and the kids nodded their heads to show that, yes, they saw it. "Ok then," he explained, "That is a little something that I call my Secret Closet of Doom. And what do you think you should do with it?"

Nobody answered. It seemed fairly obvious what he had in mind. "You leave it alone! Some of the things in there could seriously injure you. Maybe even kill you. I don't even want to discuss them in detail, because even that would probably give you nightmares for decades to come. And then you'd be just plain embarrassed. Imagine being thirty-five years old and waking up screaming in the night because your second grade teacher described the terrifying contents of a closet to you."

As you'd imagine, this made quite an impression on the second graders. They had no idea that their first day of school would involve being threatened, let alone by the teacher. In any event, after a warning like that, nobody felt too curious about the closet at all.

Around this time, Tommy had finished writing the schedule. "Not bad," said Mr. Ocean, "Here's your reward." He handed over a piece of gum, but there was a problem.

"Wait a minute!" said Tommy. "This gum is made by Chew-Rite: they're not even in business anymore! My dad said he used to chew this stuff when he was a kid! And he said it was lousy back then, too!"

"Hmm," thought Mr. Ocean, "I guess you're right, that is pretty old gum. Hey, I think that actually makes it an antique! It might be worth some serious money! Give it back!"

"No way," said Tommy. "I don't really want it, but its still mine, after all." For a minute it looked like a real standoff- Tommy and Mr. Ocean just stared at each other without saying a word. The kids weren't sure how things were going to go. Finally Mr. Ocean blinked and said, "Eh, keep it kid, you earned it, after all."

To the rest of the kids, this was just plain confusing: Mr. Ocean *did* let Tommy keep the gum, after all, but it was actually a pretty crappy piece of gum, so it wasn't really a loss for Mr. Ocean. And he had promised it to Tommy, so even *saying* he might take it back wasn't exactly the act of a nice guy. So, had Mr. Ocean done something nice? Of course not.

"Part of second grade is doing homework," announced Mr. Ocean. That means math worksheets, spelling practice, and whatever else I think up. And that includes this."

Mr. Ocean removed a large, heavy sack from his closet, and with great effort, he pulled it over to his desk. "Please come up one at a time for your hammers," he requested.

Annabelle was perplexed. "Why? I'm not a carpenter. My dad is, but he's already got a hammer. He calls it Lightning because it never strikes the same place twice."

"That's a good one," said Mr. Ocean. "Wish I'd thought of it. Anyway, the hammers are so you can do homework. You know, do some work on your home. If you see something that needs to be fixed, like a nail to pound in, do it".

The kids were confused.

"Do you really expect us to fix up our own houses?" asked Big Anthony, who certainly hoped so.

"Of course!"

"Well, how will you know if we did it or not?"

"Ah, that's the beauty of my system," replied Mr. Ocean. "I'll stop by everybody's house once in a while and have a look around. It'll be a surprise, so that way it'll keep you on your toes. I usually plan my inspections for around 6 o'clock."

"But that's dinner time," protested Israel.

"Oh, is it?" said Mr. Ocean in mock surprise. "Well, I do like a free meal from time to time."

Hammers in hand, the kids were speechless. It didn't seem like Mr. Ocean was kidding. If he was telling the truth, he was definitely living up to his reputation as a world-class cheapo.

♥ ♥ ♥

A few minutes later, an announcement came over the loudspeaker, requesting that everyone meet in the auditorium for an assembly will be held at 10:00 am to introduce the new principal. The kids automatically looked up on the wall above the door to find the clock and see what time it was, since that was where the clocks often were positioned in their classrooms in the past. This time, however, no one could find a clock. There was, however, a clock-sized circle where the paint was a slightly different color, and there was a screw and a wire poking out of the wall inside the circle.

"Hey!" said Israel. "Is that where the clock was?"

"Yeah, let me guess," murmured Mabel sarcastically, "You sold the clock too!"

Mr. Ocean looked away and pretended not to hear. "If any of you kids wear watches, you can be our official timekeepers. Your job will be to let us know when the schedule tells us know that it is time to change to a new activity." A bunch of the kids wore watches, and the rolled their eyes- who wanted extra work? Not them.

"And don't let me forget the reward for being a timekeeper," said Mr. Ocean. This got everybody's attention. "I'll pay each of you in gum."

The response from the kids was not enthusiastic. It was not exactly their idea of a delicious reward.

♥   ♥   ♥

A little later in the day, Joanna noticed that the smartboard was gone. "He probably sold it," she whispered to Annabelle.

"Ha," said Annabelle. "I bet that's the last we'll ever see of it!"

Chapter Three

Later that day, something happened that would change the whole rest of the school year for Mr. Ocean and his class. The kids were settling into the auditorium for the assembly, and the new principal was seated in a chair up on stage. The school secretary stood on stage in front of a microphone. After she cleared her throat loudly, the kids all quieted down.

"Good morning, students, and welcome back to Wasatch Arts Academy. Our motto here, as you returning students know, is that "Life is Art, and Art is Life". We are, of course, the only Arts school in the entire city, and it is what makes us so unique. Anyway, it is my pleasure to introduce our new principal, Mrs. Stabler." With this, the new principal stood up and waved.

"Did she say 'Stapler'?" Suzie said to Mabel, who was sitting next to her. Most of the other kids wondered the same thing.

"And now, we have an important tradition to observe. It is not often that a school gets a new principal, but when it happens, we like to present him or her with the 'key to the school'." She held up a large plastic key- it was the about the size of a guitar- and informed the students that it didn't actually open the doors at the school, but that it was a sort of symbol.

"To make things official, we ask the teacher who has been part of the school community the longest to present the new principal with the key. That's our special Wasatch way of bringing things full circle. And because it is such as special occasion, we have asked a few tv reporters to come and film it for us. You'll be able to watch the ceremony on the news tonight with your parents!"

An uncomfortable silence filled the auditorium. Everybody looked at everybody else; something was supposed to happen, but nobody seemed to be in charge. Finally Suzie whispered to Mr. Ocean, "I think they're talking about you! You're supposed to get up on stage!"

"Who, me?" mumbled a distracted Mr. Ocean.

Five more minutes, Mabel thought to herself, and I bet he would have been fast asleep.

"Yes, get up there!" urged Suzie.

"Oh, right, right. Of course." Mr. Ocean finally stumbled up toward the stage and stood awkwardly next to the new principal. Eager to see things move along, the secretary frowned at Mr. Ocean and thrust the key into his hands. He quickly handed it to Mrs. Stabler, and the tension was broken. "Whew!" thought Mr. Ocean, but unfortunately for him, it wasn't over yet.

"Welcome Mrs. Stapler!" he announced loudly, in an attempt to get on the new principal's good side. Mispronouncing her name, however, was not exactly the right way to go about it. Kids all around the auditorium giggled at his mistake.

And then things got really crazy. At just that moment, a janitor on the other side of the auditorium opened a door, and a huge breeze blew in. It was such a strong wind, in fact, that it blew Mr. Ocean's massive beard up over his head. His face was completely hidden. Uncovered, however, was his t-shirt, which has previously been obscured behind his bushy beard. All of the teachers gasped in shock, and all of the kids laughed in surprise when they saw what it said:

"I'm with Stupid"

To make matters worse, it had an arrow on it, and the arrow pointed directly to Mrs. Stabler. The tv reporters and the camera operators couldn't believe it- now this was the kind of news people didn't see every day! They knew that they would have a record number of viewers that night!

Total chaos overtook the auditorium. Mrs. Stabler screamed at the teachers, the teachers screamed at the kids, and finally everybody got out of the auditorium en route to their classrooms.

"And you!" huffed Mrs. Stabler to Mr. Ocean on the way out, "I won't forget this!" And she stormed off, shoving a reporter who was trying to interview her.

"I wonder what her problem was," mumbled Mr. Ocean.

"Are you kidding me?" asked Tommy. "She's

Chris Gleason

furious about your t-shirt."

"What about it? It's my favorite shirt."

"Um, she was mad about the words on it."

"Oh. I never really noticed them. I saw it at the Thrifty Saver for $1 and I really liked the color."

The kids shook their heads. How could Mr. Ocean be so absent-minded?

"I've got an idea for you," said Joanna, "And maybe it'll keep you out of trouble on the days when you wear that shirt. How about you just tuck your beard into your belt?"

"Say, that's a good idea!" he said agreeably. He immediately did so, and it turned out to be a habit that would stick.

Meet Mr. Ocean

Chris Gleason

Chapter Four

The next day, the timekeepers raised their hands at 11:15 and let Mr. Ocean know that it was time for recess. Finally! The kids raced onto the playground and got right into their favorite activities. Some of the kids liked to use the jump ropes, some worked on swinging across the monkey bars, and others played soccer on the grass.

Mabel, who was still hoping that Mr. Ocean wouldn't turn out to be a total dud as a teacher, asked him to come play on the swings. She had fond memories of her old first grade teacher, Mrs. Golfing, pushing the kids on the swings while they all laughed and laughed.

"What am I supposed to do?" said Mr. Ocean grumpily.

"Well, it's a swing set. You know, one person sits and the other person pushes. Its super fun!"

"Ok," sighed Mr. Ocean, and he plopped down onto the swing. "I'm ready." Mabel stared: this was not what she had had in mind. Well, she thought, I'll give him a good long turn, and then we can switch and I'll get a long turn being pushed. I guess that'll work out. Unfortunately, she had expected a bit too much from Mr. Ocean. After about fifteen minutes of being pushed, Mabel asked Mr. Ocean to switch. "Its only fair!" she said.

"Nah, I'm too tired. I think I'll just sit here. Getting pushed was pretty fun but now I'm kind of tired. I'll see you later on." Mabel's jaw dropped: what kind of person- let alone a teacher!- couldn't be bothered to take turns on a swing? And he was heavy- she was tired out from pushing his big old body! She growled and walked away. There was nothing she could do about it, but she wasn't going to forget this!

Some other kids had equally unimpressive experiences. Tommy and Israel asked him to play on the slide with them, but he was either to lazy or too uninterested to climb up the ladder. So, they carried him up so that he could slide down. A small group of girls was working on swinging their way across the monkey bars, and they asked him to try. He said sure, but he insisted that the girls grab his legs and lift him up while he went across "using" his arms.

At the end of recess everybody agreed on one thing: Mr. Ocean was definitely no fun on the playground.

Meet Mr. Ocean

Chapter Five

It turned out that the playground wasn't the only place that Mr. Ocean's laziness emerged. It all started when he decided his chair was uncomfortable. This surprised the kids, because it looked pretty cushiony to them- after all, they sat on hard plastic seats all day! The next day, Mr. Ocean brought in a rocking chair- complete with a thick cushion to sit on- from home.

"Oh my!" he moaned, "This changes everything! I should've done this decades ago. You just haven't lived until you've had a nice, comfy rocking chair in your classroom." All morning long, he rocked back and forth, interrupting lessons occasionally to describe how amazing it felt. Near lunchtime, however, he was singing a different tune.

"Boy are my arms tired!" he grumped. "There's no way I can push this thing all the time."

"Why don't you go to the gym and lift some weights?" suggested Big Anthony. Then you'll get strong enough to rock it as much as you want."

"No way! That sounds like a lot of work!"

Mr. Ocean sat back, motionless in the chair, and thought for a minute. "Ok, he announced. I've got a new system. I want to make sure that all of you kids are behaving properly at all times. That will help everyone to learn without distractions. That sounds reasonable, right?"

The kids nodded, wondering what the next part of the plan might be.

"Ok then, any kids who behave badly will need to come up and rock my chair for thirty minutes." He smiled, proud of his plan to get somebody else to do his work for him.

There was only one problem with this approach, however. Actually, it was a big problem, at least for Mr. Ocean. It totally backfired. From that moment on, nobody in the class misbehaved. Kids always raised their hands to talk, no one was late getting to class, and nobody even thought about cheating on tests.

"Well that didn't work out!" groused Mr. Ocean. "I'd rather have some bad behavior than rock my own chair. Oh well, I guess I'll just take this stupid rocking chair home and go back to my old chair. Maybe I'll just get a thicker cushion to sit on. That might help."

The kids couldn't help but smile- finally, they'd managed to outsmart their cranky old teacher.

♥ ♥ ♥

Some of the kids' daily work was done individually or in small groups at their desks. This meant that they sometimes finished ahead of the other kids. This wasn't a necessarily a bad thing, but the kids who finished early often made a lot of noise and fooled around, which distracted the ones who were still working.

"All right, I've had just about enough fooling around," said Mr. Ocean one day. "From now on, anyone who is done early will spend some time contributing to and/or working on the class booger sculpture."

"What?" shrieked Joanna, greatly alarmed.

"You're kidding," challenged Israel. "There's no such thing as a class booger sculpture.

Without saying a word, Mr Ocean walked to his Secret Closet of Doom, unlocked the door, and came out wheeling a small cart. On top of the cart was a slimy green and yellow sculpture about the size of a large cat, or maybe a small dog.

"Ewwwww!" the kids screamed all at once. They had never seen anything so gross in their lives.

Even Big Anthony, who secretly ate his boogers at every possible opportunity, thought it was a bit much.

"Yup," said Mr. Ocean, "I've had this for a long, long time. Every year, kids have been contributing to it. It gets bigger every year. Its nice to know you're really contributing to a work of art that might just outlive us all."

By this point, the kids were seriously freaked out.

"Does he really expect us to touch that thing?" Suzie whispered to Joanna.

"I have an idea," said Annabelle, "How about we just get a book and read quietly instead?"

"Well," said Mr. Ocean, "I guess that would be ok too. I'll tell you what, its your choice. If you finished working early, then you can either get a book or you can work on the booger sculpture. Deal?"

The kids all agreed it was a deal. Not surprisingly, none of the kids who finished early, from the day on, chose to work on the booger sculpture. They came to enjoy their time reading quietly.

After school, when the kids had left for the day, Mr. Ocean dumped the sculpture into the trash. "When I saw that week-old leftover banana flavored Jello in the cafeteria refrigerator, I knew I'd find a use for it." He chuckled to himself. "It sure is nice to know I can still fool a bunch of seven-year-olds once in a while."

Meet Mr. Ocean

Chapter Six

Having heard about so many of the oddball things that Mr. Ocean did, you may have been wondering about one very important question: how do the kids actually learn anything with such a weird teacher in charge of the classroom? Well, it turned out that Mr. Ocean wasn't actually so bad when it came to the basics of teaching. He answered kids' questions fairly well, explained new ideas ok, and his tests were pretty short. The kids suspected that he gave short tests because he was too lazy to correct longer ones, but they didn't mind. Strangely enough, though, this wasn't the only way that he showed just how lazy he was.

Remember when Tommy had to write the schedule on the board on the first day? Well, sometime in early October- about a month into the school year- Mr. Ocean had what he considered to be a terrific idea. Not surprisingly, the kids felt just the opposite.

"Class," he said once everybody had gotten settled into their seats after P.E. "I have a small announcement to make. As some of you may know, my handwriting is not the greatest. And I am deeply concerned that it might make learning difficult for you. As your teacher, it is my responsibility to make sure that you are able to learn your lessons. And so, it is with great regret that I will no longer have to- I mean, be able to!- write on the chalkboard."

The kids took in this new information. Annabelle was immediately skeptical. "Aren't you just doing this because you don't feel like getting up to write on the board? After all, that's what happened with the school schedule."

Mr. Ocean had a shocked expression on his face. "Why, Annabelle, I have no idea what you mean? This is all about you, my precious students. People ask all the time, 'Would someone think of the children?' And so this time I decided to do the right thing- to think of the children."

By now, everybody had decided that Mr. Ocean was definitely full of baloney. There was, however, still one question left to answer.

"In this case, then, who will write on the chalkboard? I mean, it is pretty handy to have things written up there so we can read them."

"That's the beauty of my new system," said Mr. Ocean proudly, "I've had some time to decide, and the five kids with the best handwriting in the class will get to do the writing for me. I mean, for you."

The five best writers- and they knew who they were without having to be called upon- blurted out, "But that's not fair! That's like giving us extra work that we don't deserve!"

"Don't worry about that," he said. "I've got a whole lot more gum. I'll pay you with that!" The newly-assigned chalkboard-writers rolled their eyes. They knew they didn't have any choice.

"We'll do it for free," said one of them. "You can keep your lousy old gum. The only thing its good for is breaking our teeth."

♥ ♥ ♥

As the days passed, things went ok for the second graders. Mr. Ocean definitely had his quirks, though, and sometimes they were pretty annoying. One of the strangest things that he occasionally did- and none of the kids had ever seen such a thing happen with their old teachers- ended up happening a couple of times a week, usually right after lunch when he'd had a big meal.

The first time it happened, it took the kids a while to even notice. They were working independently on a math worksheet, and Israel glanced up at Mr.

Ocean, intending to ask him a question about subtraction. At first he couldn't believe his eyes, but he quickly realized that what he saw was real, all right. Mr. Ocean was leaning back in his chair, with his head kind of flopped over to the side a little bit. His chin was tucked down onto his thick white beard, his eyes were closed, and a thin stream of drool drizzled from the corner of his mouth.

"Mr. Ocean!" he shouted. "Are you awake?"

Strangely, Mr. Ocean never even stirred. "What the heck is wrong with him?" asked Israel.

"I'm pretty sure he's dead," said Tommy, who had been watching too many scary movies lately. "I think this is the part where he turns into a mutant ninja zombie werewolf! Or maybe a unicorn." He had also been watching (secretly) some My Little Pony videos with his younger sister.

"He's just sleeping," said Mabel. "That's actually how my grandpa is, too," said Mabel, "Once he's out, we just have to wait for him to wake up on his own. Luckily my grandpa doesn't do it at work, though, because he's a bus driver!"

The kids chatted about what to do. They could report him to the principal, but they figured the

Principal wouldn't be able to do anything either, and they weren't so mad at him that they really wanted to get him in trouble. They decided to just see how it went.

It actually went just fine. Annabelle was the best in the class at math, so the kids asked her questions if they had any, and about twenty minutes later, Mr. Ocean woke right up. He seemed a little confused for a minute, and the kids thought it was a little gross that he didn't try to wipe the drool out of his beard, but the experience wasn't bad on the whole. Tommy summarized what everybody seemed to be feeling: "Mr. Ocean's a pretty good teacher, when he's sleeping."

Or as Big Anthony put it, "At least you know he won't cause you any problems when he's taking a nap!"

When it happened in the future, the class reacted calmly and simply handled matters themselves. For example, Mabel, the best speller in the class, gave the practice spelling test one time while Mr. Ocean slept right through it. It was an ususual solution, but then again, it was an usual situation to begin with.

❦ ❦ ❦

One morning, a cheerful woman walked in introduced herself as the new student teacher.

"I'm Ms Crumb," she said brightly. She was, young, since was still in college, and very enthusiastic, because she was still young. Mr. Ocean was outraged.

"What!" he exclaimed, "I didn't ask for a student teacher! The old principal and I had an arrangement: no student teachers!"

"Well, I don't know what to say," said Ms. Crumb, "I'm just following Principal Stabler's instructions."

"I bet its because Principal Stapler doesn't trust Mr. Ocean to get his job done!" said Big Anthony.

"Well, I refuse to cooperate!" said Mr. Ocean, "I've got a certain routine around here, and I can't have any nosy student teachers getting in the way."

This mysterious comment made the kids wonder. "Do you mean our daily class routines, Mr. Ocean?" asked Suzie.

"No!" said Mr. Ocean hastily, "I'm talking about my personal routines!" As soon as he said this, he looked like he regretted it. He had apparently spoken without thinking.

No one knew what he was talking about, only that the new student teacher had inadvertently touched a nerve.

"Fine," said Ms. Crumb, who was beginning to feel a bit less chagrined. "I was told that there is also an opening for a fourth grade student teacher." With that, she exited, leaving the kids a bit confused. And a least a few of them were disappointed.

"There went our chance to maybe have a bit more of a normal classroom," thought Annabelle with a sigh.

Meet Mr. Ocean

Chapter Seven

Every October, the PTA (short for the Parent-Teacher Association, which is a group of parents who work together with the teachers to help out the school in various ways) organized a book fair. This was a very exciting time for all the students, no matter what grade: they were all sent home with a colorful catalog of books that are available at pretty reasonable prices. After talking it over with their parents, they hopefully get to buy one or more books of their choosing. It is great for everybody because it gives kids fun new stuff to read, and the school gets to make some money that they can use to help run the school. It is a pretty common kind of thing that happens in schools all over the country.

Mr. Ocean handed out the catalogs, just like all the other teachers. "And tell your parents to send in as much money as they can!" he urged. "I mean, tell them to let you get as many books as you want. For educational purposes, of course." The kids noticed the odd way he said it, like he was trying to cover something up, but they didn't think too much of it at the time. They were far too interested in flipping through the pages of the catalog and deciding what to ask for.

A few days later, the students brought in their parents' money, and the kids began to play "the waiting game". Every day they ran breathless into the classroom, hoping the books would've arrived. "It takes time," Mr. Ocean assured them.

After about three weeks, it seemed that their time had finally come. When Mr. Ocean's students walked through the halls on their way to the classroom, they saw plenty of kids in other classes reading brand new, shiny books.

"Yippeee!" said Israel. "Today's the day!"

But disappointment awaited the kids as they entered Mr. Ocean's room.

"Where are our books?" asked Mabel eagerly.

"Um, I guess they didn't arrive yet," murmured Mr. Ocean, looking away. "I'm sure they'll be here tomorrow, though."

The kids didn't understand, but all they could do was try and trust their strange old teacher. Hopefully tomorrow would bring better news.

♥ ♥ ♥

When the kids came in the next day, they rushed up to Mr. Ocean's desk. He pulled out a large cardboard box from behind his desk. "Ok!" he announced, "Today's your lucky day!"

The kids felt an enormous wave of relief ease over them. Finally!

Mr. Ocean reached in to the box and handed a book to Suzie, a book to Tommy, and book to Israel, and a book to Annabelle. That was as far as he got, though, before they interrupted him.

"Hey!" shouted Annabelle, "These aren't the books we ordered! And, they're not even new! Mine has half the cover missing!"

"Uhhhhh...." stammered Mr. Ocean.

"What's going on here, anyway?" accused Suzie.

"Well, ok, I guess this didn't work out the way I was hoping it would," admitted Mr. Ocean, sitting down in his chair. "See, when all that money came in for the book orders, I guess I got a little greedy. I thought maybe I could just go to the Thrifty Saver and buy some books for a dime each and substitute them for the ones you ordered. It would've given me a tidy profit, since the ones you ordered cost three or four dollars each. I figured you might not even notice, since you ordered them weeks and weeks ago."

"What kind of boneheads do you think we are?" demanded Joanna.

"Well, I guess you're more observant than I was hoping," said Mr. Ocean.

"Mr. Ocean, I'm telling my parents. Of all the weird stuff you've done, this is just the worst! And my parents are going to complain to Principal Stabler and you'll probably lose your job!" Big Anthony's threat seemed to scare Mr. Ocean a little. Which was probably a good thing.

"Ok, ok!" protested Mr. Ocean. "Let's not get hasty. I actually do have your books. When I got the money, I placed the order just like I was supposed to. When they came in yesterday, ready for delivery like the other classes', I decided to wait a day so that I could run to the Thrifty Saver after school. I was hoping that I could do the old switcheroo today, and then I could return the books to the book fair company and pocket the money. "

"Anyway," he continued, "Come over when I call your name and I'll give you your book." With that, he went to his Secret Closet of Doom, unlocked the door, and came out with a box that contained the books the students had actually ordered.

"Its about time!" they cheered.

"And there's something else," said Annabelle smugly. "By my calculations, Mr. Ocean, you probably lost around five dollars on these shenanigans by buying all those crappy old books. Hopefully that teaches you a lesson, Mr. Ocean!"

With a pained look on his face, Mr. Ocean opened his mouth to reply. However, he couldn't- for once he was actually speechless.

Chapter Eight

Right after school, Mrs. Stabler called Mr. Ocean down to the office. "I've been hearing rumors," she began, "Of you being a little bit of an oddball. As far as I can tell, you haven't done anything that has crossed the line, but I want you to know, I've got my eye on you."

Mr. Ocean didn't respond to her concerns. "Is that all?" he asked.

Mrs. Stabler raised an eyebrow. "No, its not. I want to see you show a little more enthusiasm for your job, a little more school spirit."

"What do you have in mind?"

"Well, as you know, the Halloween Carnival is coming up. It is the biggest fundraiser of the year for the school. The kids pay five dollars each to enter, and the money helps run the school."

As a matter of fact, he didn't know any of this, because he wasn't the kind of teacher who kept track of important school events. But he didn't let that slip out.

"So, I've decided that I want you to participate this year."

"How?"

"Well, every year, I've heard that there's a big
Haunted House, and that the kids can walk through
it and get scared by the teachers, who have set
up various scary things. For example, a popular
trick every year is to fill a bowl with cold
spaghetti and make the kids feel it. Tell them its
brains, and it scares the heck out of them!"

"Great, that's what I'll do! I can make spaghetti!
Will the school cover the cost of the spaghetti?"

"Sorry, that was just an example, and its already
taken. One of the fourth grade teachers is going
to do it. You'll need to come up with something on
your own. And you have to pay for the materials
yourself. This is a fundraiser, after all."

Mr. Ocean frowned. The extra work of having to
think up his own idea wasn't exactly his style. And
it sounded like he was going to have to get
creative- he'd need to come up with a project
that didn't require spending money on materials.
Rats.

"And, Mr. Ocean? I've got one more thing to say-
since we're in private, I want to let you know
something: you have terrible breath. Maybe you
should get some mints or something."

• • •

The Haunted House was held in the gym every year, although the parents worked so hard to transform it that you really wouldn't even recognize it. A number of parents worked to set up large sheets of wood that made a series of rooms that the kids would walk through, sort of like a maze, and each room held its own special spooky surprise. Creepy music played, and the whole room was almost completely dark.

Annabelle and Joanna walked from room to room, getting more and more scared as they went. Near the end of the tour, they came into a room that had a black lace curtain hanging from the ceiling down to the floor. There was a sign- "Behind this curtain is a dead body. We can't show it to you- it would be far too scary. But you can smell its rotting flesh if you step up to the curtain and take a sniff."

"I don't know about this," said Joanna. "I'm already pretty freaked out as it is."

"Me too," agreed Annabelle, "But we HAVE to try it!" Bravely, they stepped up to the curtain and inhaled. The smell was absolutely gross, and they jumped back.

"Ewwww! I can't believe they found a dead body for the haunted house!" screamed Joanna. Both girls ran out in horror, and more kids entered to take their turn.

The next morning in school, the kids were all talking about the Haunted House. It was widely agreed that smelling a dead body was the most popular part by far. Mr. Ocean smiled when he heard this. "Who would've guessed," he thought to himself, "That having bad breath would come in so handy?"

Smell the

dead body

if you dare!

Chapter Nine

By late November, the weather had finally turned really cold, and Mr. Ocean had to admit that it was time to buy a new coat. His old one was in terrible shape, and it just wasn't warm enough. However, his tightwad instincts kicked in, and he just couldn't bear to spend any money. Walking down the hall, however, he got an idea that would lead to one of his worst moments of the entire year.

He saw a few 6th grade boys walking around, and he noticed that one of them was nearly as tall as he was. Even better, the boy had a thick, jacket that looked pretty warm. He waited for the boys to go into their classroom, and for the hall to be empty of witnesses. And then he- you guessed it- stole the jacket from the boy's locker. He put it on immediately- it fit fairly well, except that the sleeves were way too short. "Oh well," he thought, "It's good enough for now."

He must've been chilly that morning, because he kept the jacket on the whole time. Unfortunately for him, he would soon be the victim of a craze that the second graders were, well, crazy about. Lately they had gotten excited about writing silly signs on pieces of paper and and trying to stick them on each others' backs with tape without being caught. They wrote things like "I wet my pants", and "I am an alien" and "I kissed my dog and I liked it".

Later, when all the trouble happened, nobody would admit to having done it, but one of the kids stuck a sign on his back that said "I love money". They all thought it was a pretty funny joke.

At lunch, Mr. Ocean ran a quick errand to the Dollar Store because he heard they were having a sale on Tupperware. Unfortunately, they had sold out so he only bought one small bowl. After leaving the store, he stood at the edge of the parking lot waiting to cross the street. At this point, the sign fell off his back and he bent down and picked it up. With his long, scraggly beard, ill-fitting coat, and the empty bowl that he held in one hand, a kindly person mistook him for a homeless man and put a dollar into the bowl. This made him more excited than he'd been in years. He took the sign- even though he wasn't sure where it had come from- and held it up so that people walking by could see it. A few more nice people gave him money, and he was super psyched. The only problem was that he had the worst timing ever: Mrs. Stabler also happened to be out running an errand on her lunch break, and she saw what certainly looked like one of her teachers all dressed up like a homeless dude trying to get money from unsuspecting passersby. She was furious.

"Meet me in my office right away!" she yelled.

Back in her office, Mrs. Stabler was furious.

"I can't fire you," she said with more than a trace of regret in her voice, "Because the school has a 'three strikes and you're out' policy with teachers. This is strike one! But I can make things pretty miserable around here for you. And if you choose to quit, well, that would be your choice." Her stare made it clear that she was hoping he'd end up quitting.

"I don't know if this has ever happened before," she continued, "But it is the best punishment that I can think of. Starting immediately, someone else will take over teaching your second grade class. Just yesterday, lunch lady Doris told me that she will be leaving soon because she's moving to a different state. So, guess what? You're going to be our new lunch lady!"

Mr. Ocean thought for a minute. His one question was not surprising, though: "Will I still get paid?"

"Yes," she Mrs. Stapler. "Legally, I can't take away

your pay. But tomorrow, instead of going to your classroom, just go to the cafeteria. That will be all." With that, she turned away and let him see himself out.

Meet Mr. Ocean

Chapter Ten

When the kids arrived in Mr. Ocean's room the next morning, someone else was sitting in his chair. "My name is Mrs. Higgins," she explained, "And I'll be your substitute."

"No Mr. Ocean?!" said Tommy. "Is he sick?"

"No," said Mrs. Higgins. "He has been given a different assignment in the school."

"What?" squealed Joanna. "He won't be our teacher anymore?"

"I'm afraid not," said the substitute. "And I've been asked not to discuss the details with you."

The children were both curious and a little disturbed- what could've happened? Where was Mr. Ocean? What had he done? Was he in trouble? The kids had lots of questions, and many theories. Annabelle guessed that he had robbed a bank or something, due to his oversized love of money. Joanna quickly pointed out, however, that that would've required a lot of work, which wasn't like him at all. A variety of possible explanations were explored throughout the morning. The kids couldn't agree on what had happened for sure, but they did agree on one thing: while he wasn't exactly the best teacher ever, they still hoped he was okay!

At lunchtime, Mr. Ocean's kids got their second surprise of the day. And it was a surprise they shared with the rest of the school. As they walked into the lunchroom, they saw Mr. Ocean in the serving area, dishing up food.

"Mr. Ocean," Israel exclaimed, "What are you doing here?"

"Oh, there was a bit of a mix up yesterday, and Mrs. Stabler is punishing me. So far, though, I have to say this isn't too bad of a job. I even brought my own apron from home." He pointed to his chest and showed off the apron, which read, in bright red letters, "Kiss the cook". "Want some spaghetti and meatballs? Its really good today!"

Israel shook his head in disbelief, and walked over to sit with the rest of the class.

As the second graders ate, they talked about what could've happened.

"I'm guessing he stole the fundraiser money from Halloween," suggested Annabelle.

"Or maybe he punched Mrs. Stapler. Those two never did get along."

Near the end of lunch, Tommy looked over at Mr. Ocean and saw something she almost couldn't believe.

"This must be my imagination," he thought. But he looked one more time, and it happened again. Mr. Ocean had just licked the serving spoon and put it back in the bowl of spaghetti. Tommy was shocked. He didn't know what to do with this information, so he decided to keep it to himself for a while.

However, Tommy wasn't the only one who saw what Mr. Ocean did. At the end of lunch, Mrs. Stabler's voice came over the loudspeaker: "Mr. Ocean, please report to my office immediately!"

When he got to the office, Mrs. Stabler began yelling at him right away. "Strike two, Mr. Ocean!"

"What do you mean?" he asked, pretending to be innocent.

"Just take a look and you'll see just what I mean." She pointed to a tv screen which showed a video of him licking the spoon.

"I knew you would screw things up," she ranted, "So I turned on the old security cameras that the old principal installed years ago. I caught you red-handed. I just didn't think it would be so gross."

"So does this mean I'll be going back to my classroom?" said Mr. Ocean.

"Ha!" said Mrs. Stabler, "No way. I'm giving you a job that even you can't screw up. Starting tomorrow, you'll be filling in someplace else. And in case you weren't sure: this was your second strike."

"Rats," he thought, "That lunch lady thing was the best job I ever had."

• • •

The next morning, Mrs. Higgins led Mr. Ocean's former students down to the gym for P.E. They were astonished by what they saw.

"Surprise!" said Mr. Ocean. "There was a bit of a 'situation' yesterday in the cafeteria, so I'm going to be your new P.E. teacher instead. Today we'll be learning about basketball."

The kids rolled their eyes. They already knew all about basketball already. "Why don't you just divide us into two teams and let us play against each other? That's what a normal P.E. teacher would do," suggested Joanna.

"Well, I'm hardly a normal P.E. teacher," said Mr. Ocean.

That's for sure, thought every kid in the room.

"Anyway, let's get started. You see that round metal circle up there in the air? That's the basketball hoop. The white part that hangs down is called the net. And this round thing on the ground is the ball." Mr. Ocean looked around to make sure everyone was taking in the main points of the lesson.

"But we know all that!" said Mabel. The kids were getting restless. The point of P.E. was to move around and get some exercise, not get lectured to about things that even a whiny little kindergartener would know.

"Hmmm, ok, then let me give you a few points on shooting baskets," Mr. Ocean said, hoping to make a good impression. He lifted the ball off the ground, struggling to hoist it up as high as his shoulder. He finally took a shot, but it only went up about two feet. He had missed the basket by at least six feet

Embarassed, he insisted that he be allowed to take another try. The second shot was also a pathetic one. So were the third, fourth, fifth, and sixth ones.

"Mr. Ocean, just let us play!" chanted the kids.

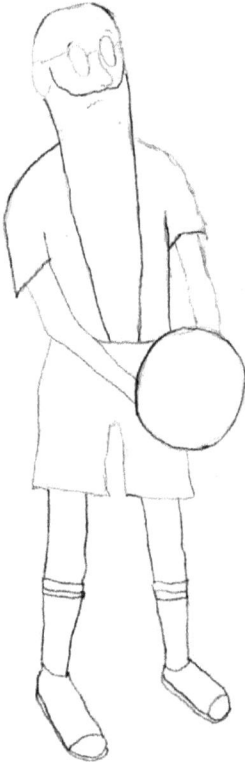

"Ok, ok," he weezed. "Just one last chance." At this point, Mr. Ocean was barely able to stand up straight. He staggered around like crazy, and when he finally took his shot, the ball zoomed straight up and hit the bottom of the basketball hoop. Then it bounced off at an unexpected angle and hit Big Anthony in the nose.

"Owwww!" he screamed. There was blood everywhere. "Is it bad?" he asked everybody.

"Umm, not too bad," replied Mr. Ocean, who was secretly panicking. "Somebody go get the school nurse!" He felt just awful; he knew he wasn't the greatest teacher ever, but actually hurting a student? That was just too much.

Moments later, the nurse arrived with icepacks and old towels. "At least it isn't broken," she announced, "But we've got a bleeder, all right!" Sobbing, Big Anthony accompanied her to the nurse's office.

"Maybe you guys should just break into two teams and play each other," decided Mr. Ocean.

"Finally!" said Mabel to Suzie under her breath.

The kids, upset by the accident and the sight of all that blood, weren't at their best, but after a few minutes they settled down and had a great game. As soon as Mrs. Higgins led the kids back to class, a voice came over the loudspeaker, "Mr. Ocean, please report to my office. Immediately!"

That's it, thought Mr. Ocean. Three strikes. I'm out. Out of a job, that is. Dejected, he trudged down to the principal's office, ready to be fired.

Once he got there, however, he was surprised with how things went. "I'm not counting this as a third strike, Mr. Ocean", said Mrs. Stabler. "Big Anthony told me it was an accident. Sometimes people get bumped around a little in P.E., and while I hate to see a student get injured, this is the kind of thing that could've happened to anyone."

Mr. Ocean was relieved. At least he'd still have a job! "So I'll stay on as the P.E. teacher?"

"No way," she said, "You're the worst P.E. teacher ever. Just imagine how many more kids could get hurt if you stayed on. I think the best choice is to send you back to your classroom. At least I can keep an eye on you there, and none of the kids should get hurt."

Mr. Ocean was happy. He hadn't particularly liked being a P.E. teacher. He would miss the lunch lady job, since it came with free food, but on second thought, it did involve a lot of standing around. At least his old classroom had a chair.

Meet Mr. Ocean

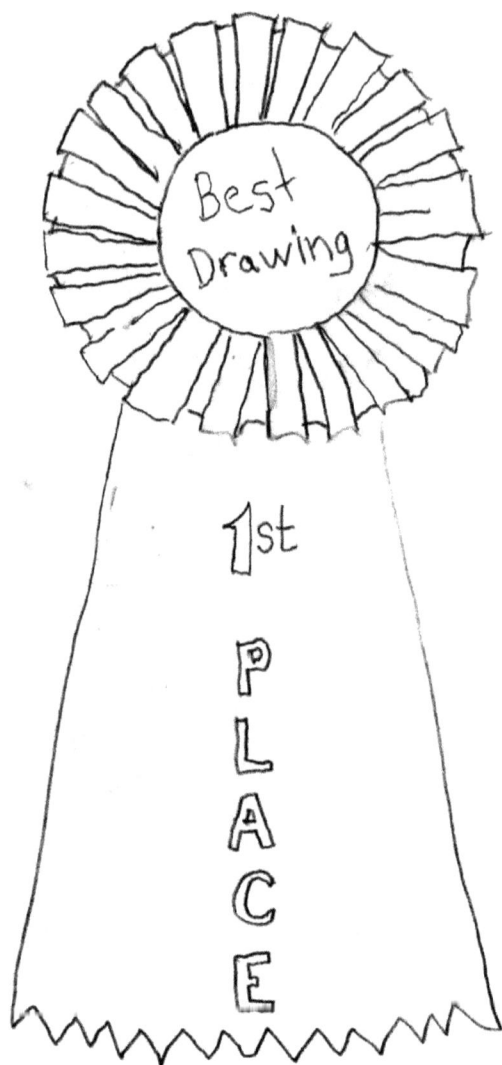

Chapter Eleven

Once Mr. Ocean got back to the classroom, things went pretty smoothly.. His normal quirks were still there, of course, but he seemed to be making an effort to be not quite as hard to deal with. As Thanksgiving grew near, he made a rather interesting announcement.

"Some of you may already know about this," he said, "But the grocery store in town has organized a contest open to children of all ages. They're asking each kid who enters to draw a picture that shows what Thanksgiving means to them. To keep it fair, they're setting it up so that only kids in the same grade are competing against each other. There are prizes for the 1st, 2nd and 3rd place. The winner will receive $100, the runner up will get $50, and third place is $25. And I have high hopes for you all, since Wasatch is arts school and you've had so much practice and experience drawing. You all have one week to bring me back your drawings."

The kids were thrilled- it seemed like a great chance to make a huge amount of money! They began discussing their drawings, and as soon as they had some free time later that day, some kids even began writing down ideas and doing sketches. For once, Mr. Ocean had had a great idea.

♥ ♥

When the students handed in their drawings a week later, Mr. Ocean was impressed. "I knew you would all do a good job," he said, "But these are even better than I expected! I'll deliver them to the grocery store this afternoon.

A week later, there was excellent news: Annabelle had won first place! In addition, Tommy and Mabel had won second and third places, respectively.

The class had a small party to celebrate; with all of the excitement, no one noticed Mrs. Stabler peering in the window, watching with great interest. "Hmmmm," she mused. "What an unusually nice thing for Mr. Ocean to do. And that's what worries me. Is there more to this story?" She found it hard not to suspect the worst, although maybe he finally had changed his ways. Time would tell.

Meet Mr. Ocean

Chapter Twelve

About a week before Christmas, Mr. Ocean walked into the classroom with a twinkle in his eye. "Notice anything new?" he asked.

The kids giggled. They never would've imagined it, but Mr. Ocean was wearing a Santa hat!

"What's up with the new hat?" asked Tommy.

"Well, I couldn't find my hat yesterday afternoon, and this bald head of mine doesn't do very well in the cold by itself. So I stopped by the Dollar Store and they had this fancy new hat on sale for only- you guessed it- a dollar." He was clearly pretty excited about his new purchase.

"Um, that's great, Mr. O," said Joanna. "Its good to see that you're feeling the holiday spirit.

♥   ♥   ♥

At the end of the day, the kids left and Mr. Ocean was all alone in the classroom. He unlocked the door to his Secret Closet of Doom, and he pulled out a black trash bag that was pretty full. "I can't believe I was able to get all these old soda cans from the teacher's lounge," he said, "I can take them to the recycling center and get at least five or six dollars for them! Maybe I'll buy myself some extra dessert for Christmas day. Mmmmm, it'll be the most delicious Christmas ever!" And to keep warm on his way home, he put on the Santa hat, of course.

As he was walking down the hallway, he went by the kindergarten rooms. Just as he passed by a bunch of kindergarteners who were standing around in the hall, he noticed that his shoe was untied, so he bent down to tie it. When he set down the bag of empty cans, one rolled out, and a fourth grade boy grabbed it and ran off. Mr. Ocean, it turned out, knew the boy all too well. It was Mabel's older brother Rudolf, and he was a real troublemaker.

"Hey!" shouted Mr. Ocean, jumping to his feet and grabbing the big bag of cans. "Rudolf!" Come back here! I've got big plans for that can. I need it to make Christmas extra special! You don't want to ruin Christmas, do you?" He ran down the hall in hot pursuit of Rudolph.

If only he had looked around him, he would've seen quite a sight, namely a group of seriously freaked out kindergarteners. And you could definitely understand why: they had just seen an old man with a long white beard, a red Santa cap, and a large bag of what certainly

could've been presents ran by their door begging "Rudolf" not to ruin Christmas. It was not the kind of thing they saw everyday.

"It's Santa!" a number of them exclaimed, and they began to chatter excitedly. One little boy got a little too excited and wet his pants, but at least it was the end of the day, so he could go right home and change.

"He's awfully skinny for Santa," one girl said skeptically. "Maybe he got that weight loss surgery," someone speculated. "Or maybe he started hitting the gym," said someone else. "I bet he cut out the carbs," said another.

One thing was for sure: they'd never forget the day Santa visited their school.

♥   ♥   ♥

Some times, Mr. Ocean was kind of an interesting guy, and sometimes he was kind of a pain in the neck. Sometimes, he was both. One thing was for sure: life with Mr. Ocean was never boring. Take, for example, the unusual incident involving the post office and a pile of spelling tests.

It was lunchtime on Friday. The kids had just taken their spelling tests, and Mr. Ocean was planning to grade them right after lunch, like he usually did. At the beginning of lunchtime, he decided to spend a few minutes finishing up his Christmas cards so he could mail them. As usual, his desk was incredibly messy, with papers everywhere. Every year, he wrote a one-page "newsletter" that he included with his Christmas card telling them what had been going in his life. It wasn't particularly interesting, and it mostly consisted of a list of the tv shows that he had watched during the past year. He also threw in a few grocery store coupons that he had clipped from the paper in an effort to be kind and considerate. It was a weird tradition, but it was his tradition, so he kept doing it year after year.

Anyway, he had a stack of the newsletters on his desk, and a stack of spelling tests next to them, and you might be able to guess what happened next. For some reason, he got mixed up and put the spelling tests into the envelopes with his Christmas cards. Then he licked the envelopes, put stamps on them, and walked two blocks to the post office. He dropped them into the mail slot and got back to school just in time to pick up the kids from lunch.

Later that afternoon, Annabelle asked, "Did you get our spelling tests graded yet?" She was a top notch speller, and always got a 100, so she was eager to see if she had done it again. Keeping the streak alive was important to Annabelle. Big Anthony groaned, because he was just the opposite: spelling was not his strong point and he never looked forward to getting his tests back.

Mr. Ocean's eyebrows shot up. He looked at his desk and realized what had happened. He panicked on the inside, but tried not to show it. To cover his mistake, he blurted out the first thing that came to his mind. "Um, yes," he lied, "You all got a B."

This earned a mixed response. The kids who usually got less than a B were thrilled, and kids like Annabelle were mad.

"Ok, ok," said Mr. Ocean. "Maybe that isn't the way to handle it."

"Handle what?" said Israel.

"Well, I somehow managed to lose your tests."

"How? Where are they?"

"Well, I know where they are, more or less, but I can't get them back."

"This doesn't make any sense," said Tommy Tibbler. "I'm going to tell Mrs. Stabler that you're losing your mind *and* losing our tests."

"No!" protested Mr. Ocean, who was worried about the dreaded third strike. "How's this- because I screwed up, I'll give you all a 100 on this week's test."

Cheers went up around the room. This was solution that everybody could live with!

Big Anthony suddenly had an idea. "Why don't you just test us again?" he almost asked. He quickly realized that he'd better keep his mouth shut. "There's no way I'd have gotten a 100 on my own, so I'm keeping my mouth shut. This is like finding money in the street!"

As usual, life with Mr. Ocean was never boring.

♥   ♥   ♥

The timekeepers that Mr. Ocean relied on for keeping the class on schedule were starting to get a little sick of the extra effort they had to put in, and they raised the subject with the rest of the kids one morning before Mr. Ocean got to the classroom.

"I know what we should do," said Mabel, "Let's get our parents to all chip in a little bit of money and buy him a watch. That way he'll be able to keep track of time on his own- like a grown-up should."

"That's a great idea," agreed Israel. "Kids usually get their teacher a gift at the holidays anyway."

So the kids carried out their plan, with Joanna's mom agreeing to take the money they raised and buy him a watch. When the time came for her to go shopping, she was surprised to see how much money they had.

"This is almost a hundred and twenty dollars!" she said.

"Yup, most of the kids had their parents donate around five dollars, so it added up pretty quick."

"Great," said her mom. "And I have another idea. How about we go to an antique store to get him a cool old watch rather than just something boring from the mall? I think he might really like that."

"Sure mom, whatever you say."

Right before the end of school on the day before Winter vacation, the kids gave Mr. Ocean his gift.

"Thanks, everybody," he said with a smile, "I'll wait until Christmas morning to open it. Have a nice vacation!"

"I hope he'll like it," said Joanna.

"I bet he will," said Mabel. "After all, its an antique- just like him."

Chapter Thirteen

When the kids came back from Winter vacation, the first thing they noticed was how happy Mr. Ocean looked.

"This watch," he said proudly, "Is the nicest gift anybody ever got me. It was really generous of you kids to spend all that money. I'll never be able to thank you enough!"

"Plus, you'll always know what time it is, so the timekeepers can go off duty!" Tommy said.

"Yup," agreed their teacher. "I guess I'm old enough to tell time for myself."

❤   ❤   ❤

Later that day, the kids made a new friend- one who would end up playing a big role in their classroom.

The kids were working on a subtraction worksheet when Suzie suddenly pointed to the window and yelled. "Look over there!" she squealed. Outside the window, a squirrel stood up on his back legs and pressed his front feet and his nose against the window like he wanted to come in. The kids were so excited that they ran over to see him.

Surprisingly, he didn't even run away.

"Why that's my old pal Chuck!" said Mr. Ocean. The kids weren't sure whether or not to believe him.

"I'm not kidding," he went on, "We've been friends for a couple of years now. You can go ahead and let him in."

Mr. Ocean's story was so weird that the kids weren't sure if they should believe it. But they certainly wanted it to be true, so they opened the window, and after a minute or so of sniffing the air, and looking around, Chuck ran in.

"Wow!" exclaimed Israel.

"We should get a picture- nobody is going to believe this!" suggested Mabel.

"Oh no," said Mr. Ocean. "No pictures. In fact, if you want Chuck to be able to come in, we have to make a deal. You can't tell anybody who isn't in our class about him, because I'm worried about Mrs. Stabler finding out. She would go crazy and I'd get into big trouble. It would be my third strike, and I'd be out of a paycheck. I mean, a job."

The kids thought it over. It seemed like a hard secret to keep, but the excitement of having a pet squirrel made it sound completely worth it.

"It's a deal!" they agreed.

The kids looked on in surpise as Chuck jumped onto Mr. Ocean's desk and ran over to a small bag of peanuts that Mr. Ocean had been snacking on. "They've always been his favorite," explained the teacher.

After eating a peanut, Chuck began to walk around the class for the next few minutes. Mr.

Ocean announced that it was time to go back to work, so Chuck would need to head back outside.

"But won't he get cold?" asked Suzie.

"Nope. After all, squirrels live outside all year long, so they're used to winter weather. At least we give him a chance to come in from the cold once in a while and have a nice little snack."

The kids couldn't disagree, and they watched excitedly as Chuck ran back outdoors. "Don't worry kids," Mr. Ocean said reassuringly, "He can come back in tomorrow. We can let him in every day for a few minutes, as long as everybody keeps the secret."

The kids were beyond thrilled. This was quite possibly the most exciting thing that any of them had ever seen. And the promise of it being an every day thing? Just unbelievable. Who would've imagined such a thing from a teacher like Mr. Ocean?

♥   ♥   ♥

Life with Mr. Ocean definitely ended up having its good points as the year went on, but that isn't to say that he suddenly improved and turned into the best teacher ever, either. One incident that showed his bad side was when the time of the year came for parent/teacher conferences. Joanna and her mom sat down with Mr. Ocean to talk about her progress during the school year.

"Your daughter," began Mr. Ocean, "Is a very bright girl. She does very well on her math tests, her homework is always handed in on time, and she is very helpful around the classroom."

"Is there anything she could work a little harder on?" asked her mom.

"Well, she could practice a bit more for her spelling tests. She is a good speller, but if she studied her words a little more often, I think she could get a one hundred on her tests most of the time."

"Is there anything else we should know?"

Mr. Ocean looked down at a paper on his desk. "Mabel is also good at science. I would encourage this interest by getting her some books from the library about science."

At this, Joanna's mom flinched. "Did you just call her Mabel?"

"Um, yes," he stuttered, "I thought that might've been her name."

"Are you kidding me?" the mom yelled. "You don't even know the name of a little girl who has been in your class the whole year?"

"Well, to be fair to me," explained Mr. Ocean, "I don't really memorize any of the kids' names. That sounds like a lot of work. But I manage to remember lots of things about them. For example, the things I told you about her school work are all true. When you get to be my age, remembering names is tough stuff!"

Joanna's mom was unhappy, but she was too busy to go down to the principal's office to make a complaint. "We'll be keeping an eye on you!" she said, storming out of the room.

Not surprisingly, the rest of the parents had pretty much the same experience. On the plus side, Mr. Ocean knew lots about the kids, including their hobbies and interests, and he kept careful track of their grades, but he was just plain lousy at remembering names. Did this make him a bad teacher? Good question. Somehow, word didn't make its way back to Mrs. Stabler about his little "memory problem".

♥   ♥   ♥

One day, Mrs. Stabler made an announcement over the loudspeaker. "Any teachers who would like earn some extra money, please come to the office after school." Naturally, Mr. Ocean hurried to the office as soon as he could.

"Sometimes our bus drivers get sick," said Mrs. Stabler to a small group of teachers, "So we need substitutes. Anybody with a valid driver's license can sign up." She groaned when she saw Mr. Ocean.

"I'm not sure I feel safe with you driving the kids

around," she said to Mr. Ocean.

"But I have a driver's license!" he said, pulling out his wallet and handing her the license for inspection.

"Hmm," she said, "I guess I can't stop you. But I'm only going to call you if all of the other substitutes are busy. Hopefully it will never come to that. And if you do end up driving, and you get into any trouble at all, that could be your third strike."

It took a while, but eventually the other substitute drivers were too busy, and the school secretary was forced to ask Mr. Ocean to drive a bus full of kids home after school. With great gusto, he hopped into the bus and began driving downtown. He was a good enough driver, but unfortunately his absentminded ways caused him a bit of a problem.

Wasatch Arts Academy

Mr. Ocean's normal afternoon routine was to drive to the library and read the newspaper, as he felt that having the newspaper delivered to his house would have been far too extravagant. On this day, he did his regular thing and parked in front of the library. With his head in the clouds, he didn't even think about the fact that he was driving a schoolbus. The kids were so shocked that they were absolutely silent as they watched him walk into the building.

About forty minutes later, he came back out to the parking lot and was confused when he couldn't find his car. He did finally notice the bus, however, when the kids' screams got his attention.

"What the heck were you doing in there?" they demanded.

"We're telling our parents!"

"You're going to get fired for this!"

Mr. Ocean realized that he had indeed made a huge mistake, and that he was facing enormous consequences. He looked across the street and saw what he hoped was the solution to his problem: Dippy Donuts! And he knew he had a coupon in his wallet for a free box of donut holes. Maybe things could work out for him after all.

"I have an idea," he announced. "Maybe we can make a deal. If you can keep a secret about my little mistake, I'll treat everybody to Dippy Donuts!"

A cheer went up throughout the bus.

"Everybody can have a donut hole, and as many free napkins as you want!" proclaimed Mr. Ocean.

A "boo" went up throughout the bus. Maybe this wasn't going to be so easy, thought the cheap old teacher.

"No way!" hollered the kids. "You've got to do better than that!"

"Ok, ok," he said, "I'll throw in a free cup of water!"

"Booooooooo! Never! That's not good enough!"

And they made a fair point: one lousy donut hole for all that inconvenience? Plus some free stuff that Dippy Donuts gave out anyway? Uh-uh. Mr. Ocean was going to have to make a better offer. After a good deal of bargaining back and forth, a compromise was reached. In exchange for their silence, each kid would receive would receive three donuts and a medium juice. Mr. Ocean nearly wept when he thought of the financial loss of almost $100, but at least he wouldn't lose his job, which would've been a much, much bigger loss.

"At least I've got this box of free donut holes," he thought to himself. I just hope I don't get sick of them. I'm going to be eating these things for breakfast, lunch, and dinner for days to come."

Meet Mr. Ocean

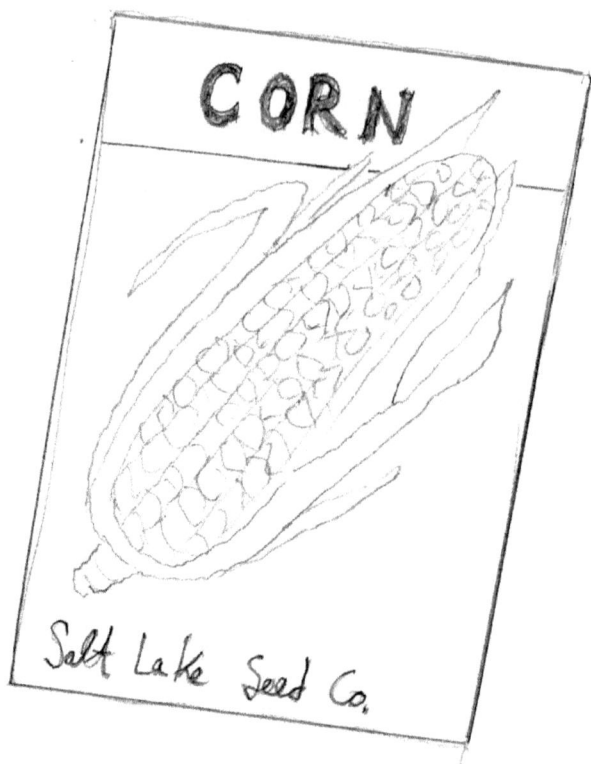

Chapter Fourteen

In February, Mr. Ocean had one of his best ideas ever. I realize that that isn't saying much, since he wasn't exactly known for having good ideas, but still, kids from all over the school thought he was a genius. He even managed to impress his old enemy Mrs. Stabler.

It all began on the day that Mr. Ocean went to Mrs. Stabler's office to discuss his idea.

"Are you feeling ok?" asked the school secretary, since Mr. Ocean usually did everything possible to avoid the principal. He certainly had never come to her office on purpose before.

"Never better!" he announced. "I've got a fantastic idea that I think the whole school would benefit from."

"Well, go right in and tell her yourself," said the secretary. "I'm sure she's in the mood for a laugh."

Face to face with Mrs. Stabler, Mr. Ocean laid out his grand plan. "Lots of schools are starting gardens," he began, "And it is a great way to teach children about where their food comes from. These days, most of what kids eat comes from a box, a bag, or a can. These youngsters don't realize that food can be grow in their own backyards. I think a school garden would also teach them about healthy eating. We could build a small greenhouse by the playground and get started in early spring."

"I like it!" declared Mrs. Stabler. "I think the parents would love it too. Why, I bet we can get some volunteers to put up the greenhouse for us. The kids could spend some time in their classrooms learning about plants, then we could all work together to plant seeds, care for the plants, and then do a big harvest where everybody gets to eat a meal in the cafeteria that we all helped grow. What an idea! I'll be famous!" With that, her eyes narrowed, and she glared at Mr. Ocean. "Unless you want to take all the credit, that is..." she said menacingly.

"Me? No!" stammered Mr. Ocean. "I don't care a bit about that. I just wanted to mention the possibility to you."

"Good!" she said eagerly. "Then I'll be in charge!"

Mr. Ocean left, and as he turned his back away from the principal, he smiled. This was working out even better than he had hoped.

The kids all spent about the next month studying plants in great detail. Even Big Anthony, who usually didn't get interested in much, had to admit it was pretty neat. Science classes were devoted to studying the life cycle of various plants, art classes were dedicated to drawing, painting, and making sculptures of plants, and music classes were given over to songs about plants. In the classroom, many poems and stories were written about plants- both their beauty and their importance. Lists of what to plant were made: everyone got to contribute their ideas based on their favorite vegetables to eat. Even the teachers were consulted. Mr. Ocean, for example, loved lettuce. Seeds were planted, and the waiting began. Even though it was chilly outside, the green house proved to be a perfect place to grow their garden.

Chapter Fifteen

Every year in March, the school held a Science Fair. It was a big deal: every kid in school chose a science project and spent a ton of time working on it. After weeks of studying, preparing, and experimenting, they would present their discoveries. The gym was used to display everyone's projects, and every kid got a small table to use to show off their stuff. Each grade had a competition, with small prizes given to the best projects.

Choosing a subject to study was usually a matter of personal taste: kids who were interested in space, for example, might study rocket ships, or planets. Big Anthony was mostly interested in video games, but he couldn't think of a way to do a science project about that. His other hobby was eating, so he came up with the idea to investigate which kinds of food get moldy the fastest. He began by using chunks of cheese, leftover fried chicken, and fish sticks, but they ended up smelling pretty bad. Mr. Ocean suggested that he try other types of bread- bagels vs. white bread, for instance. So he used English muffins, wheat bread, French bread, sesame seed bagels, and white bread. His discovery? That they all went moldy at about the same time. Not very interesting, really, and it wasn't clear to anyone what it might've proved that was at all useful, but it was a discovery nonetheless. For Big Anthony, who was a C-student on a good day, it was a fairly big victory.

However, things unfortunately took a turn for the worse on the day that of the science fair. Big Anthony, like all the other kids, had brought his project in from home and was planning to go set it up in the gym fairly soon. As was often the case, Chuck the squirrel was hanging out in the classroom, walking around and checking to see if the kids had brought in anything he might be interested in. There were really only two things that Chuck might've been interested in- a girl squirrel, and food. Unfortunately for Big Anthony, Chuck seemed to consider chunks of moldy bread to be a pretty good food source. While Big Anthony was over in the corner looking at a model of a human heart that Tommy Tibbler had made from Legos, Chuck was chowing down on Big Anthony's project. When Big Anthony came back to his desk, he saw Chuck eating the last chunk of bread.

Important science:
which kind of bread
gets moldy the fastest?
by Big Anthony

"Oh no!" cried Big Anthony. "I can't believe he ate my moldy bread!"

"Ewwww," said Annabelle. "Gross!"

"Do you think he's going to barf?" asked Joanna.

The kids crowded around Chuck and Big Anthony. None of them had ever seen a squirrel barf before, and it seemed like were about to get the chance.

"A barfing squirrel," shouted Israel. "Now that's a great science fair project!"

As it happened, Chuck didn't barf- at least not inside the classroom. Mr. Ocean quickly shooed him outside, where he may or may not eventually have barfed.

Big Anthony looked ready to cry.

"My project is ruined!" he moaned.

"Well," said Mr. Ocean, "You still have the poster that you drew which explains everything. You just need some moldy bread."

With that, he began stroking his beard. It was not uncommon for him to do this while he was deep in thought. As he did, Joanna noticed a crumb pop out from the long, white hairs.

"I've got an idea!" she said. "Mr. Ocean, your beard is so big that I bet you've got a million crumbs in there. And they've probably been there forever- you probably have crumbs in there that are old enough to drive a car!"

"Hmmm," he said, stroking his beard again. A couple more crumbs popped out.

"Here's a cardboard box," said Tommy, "If you comb your beard out, I bet you could use it to collect the crumbs!"

"Good idea," said Mr. Ocean. "Glad to help out." In truth, Mr. Ocean felt a little bad about Chuck's destructive appetite, and he figured his beard was long overdue for some grooming. He began to comb his beard, and the crumbs rained down into the box. After a while, a huge pile had accumulated.

"And now," he said, "Somebody get me some glue." Moments later, he began gluing together small piles of crumbs so that they looked, more or less, like chunks of bread.

"And now," he said, "I need green paint, and a small brush." He then started to dab paint on the chunks of bread very carefully so that it looked like mold.

"Wow," said Mabel, "That is the weirdest thing I have ever seen. But, I think its going to work!"

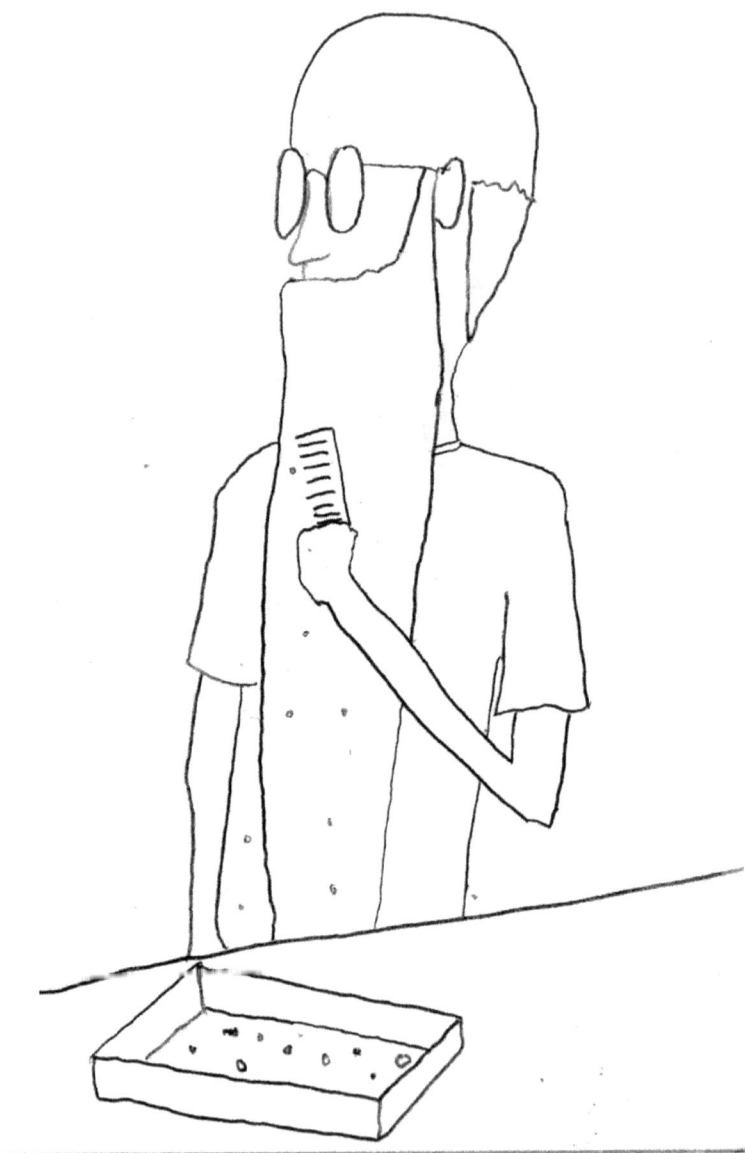

Big Anthony, who had been looking on like an expectant father waiting for a baby to be born, shouted, "Yippee!" when Mr. Ocean finally set down his brush. "Good as new!"

As the kids carried their projects down to the gym to get ready for the science fair, they agreed on two things: that Big Anthony's project was pretty disgusting, and that Mr. Ocean had really saved the day.

♥ ♥ ♥

Thanks to careful watering and good soil preparation, the school garden was growing like a weed. Well, not a weed, of course, because the kids had carefully removed any weeds the minute they were spotted poking up through the soil- but like plants that you'd actually *want* to eat. After a month, the first lettuces were ready to be harvested. Mrs. Stabler announced over the loudspeaker that the cafeteria would serve some lettuce the next day for everyone to get to try.

Near the end of lunchtime, the lunch lady took some kids outside to get some lettuce. They found, however, that some of it had disappeared! Where big, green leaves had grown, small, stubby plants remained.

When the kids came back from lunch, they saw a bowl on Mr. Ocean's desk, and it was almost empty—there was just a little bit of salad left in the bottom.

"Mr. Ocean!" exclaimed Tommy. "Did you steal our lettuce?"

"Um, why do you say that?" asked Mr. Ocean, his eyes shifting from left to right. "Just because I enjoy salad, you can't assume that I stole the lettuce!"

"But you said last month when we were studying plants how much you love lettuce, and now our lettuce is gone, and I think you stole it!"

"Stole it?" said Mr. Ocean. "Even if I had harvested the lettuce, and I'm not saying I did, the lettuce belonged to the whole school, which I am part of. Therefore, the lettuce did technically belong to me. You can't "steal" something that already belongs to you, can you?"

This was confusing, and it seemed like Mr. Ocean was trying to weasel his way out of things, but the kids couldn't really say his explanation sounded wrong, either. Worse yet, there was no actual way to prove whether or not Mr. Ocean had really taken their lettuce.

"Anyway, class, this is a good time to teach you all what happens to lettuce when you harvest lettuce. If you cut it with scissors, it just grows back, so there will be more later. This is what we in the business call a real teachable moment."

The kids thought about this. That the lettuce would grow back did sound like a bit of a silver lining. But still...

"And there's one more thing that I think you kids should remember: whose idea was this garden, anyway? Mine. That's right, if it weren't for me, you wouldn't even have a school garden in the first place. Maybe losing a little bit of lettuce is a small price to pay for getting to have the garden. Think of it as interest on a loan."

The kids didn't know what "interest on a loan" meant, but they understood his overall point. "So you're saying we should just let you eat our lettuce whenever you feel like it?" said Joanna huffily.

"I'm saying that that would be a nice way to thank me for helping to get the garden organized in the first place. And anyway, let's move on. Everybody take out your math worksheets and we'll start at the top."

This was a frustrating moment for the kids- they knew who did it, but they couldn't prove it.

Meet Mr. Ocean

This is a Bill
Date: Today
Amount: $86.00

For educational purposes,
I am requesting this
small amount of money.
You _do_ want quality

teaching for your child,
right?

signed,
Mr. Ocean

Chapter Sixteen

After a couple of days, the kids had forgotten about the lettuce incident. They were having so much fun with Chuck in the classroom that they didn't even think about holding a grudge against their teacher. Having spent months and months and months in his class, they practically expected him to do weird stuff on a more or less daily basis, after all.

In early April each year, another beloved tradition took place: the annual Spring Concert. The music teacher kicked things into overdrive and got the kids to practice their singing until it was just fantastic. The school band got their instruments perfectly tuned up, and they too practiced like never before. By the time of the concert, everyone sounded terrific.

The concert happened on a Friday night, and everybody dressed up for it. It was open to the community, and even people who had no connection to the school showed up, just because the entertainment was so enjoyable. Each class got up on stage and performed two songs, then the next class took their place.

Mrs. Stabler walked around the edges of the

auditorium, just as proud as could be- after all, these were her students! She shook hands, greeted people, and accepted congratulations on running such a fine school. "How lucky we all are to have an arts school like Wasatch!" she often heard. Her mood was great until she saw Mr. Ocean standing at the back of the room holding up a microphone.

"What are you doing?" she hissed.

"Um, recording the concert."

"What for?"

This seemed to stump him for a minute, then he came up with a reply.

"Because I might like to listen to it later. After all, you can't deny how amazing these kids sound."

Mr. Stabler considered this. "I suppose you're right. The kids are putting on a fantastic show. Carry on." And she moved on to greet more parents and accept congratulations for how well things were going.

Mr. Ocean wiped the sweat from his brow. She had bought his story! Whew! But what did he have in mind? Nobody knew but him.

❤ ❤ ❤

As Spring continued, the kids enjoyed the warmer weather outside. Inside the classroom, things went on pretty much as usual. That is to say, you never knew what you were going to get with Mr. Ocean. The one thing the kids knew they could count on was that things would never be boring.

In Math, Mr. Ocean had been teaching the kids a bit

about how to manage money- how to save money, how banks work, and what taxes were for.

"What are taxes?" asked Annabelle on the day he began the lesson.

"Well," said Mr. Ocean, "Grown ups have to pay part of the money they earn every year to the government so that the government has money for things that we all use. Does anyone have any ideas about what kind of things that might be?"

"How about libraries?" asked Mabel.

"Right!"

"What about parks?" asked Israel.

"Yup."

"Maybe schools?" asked Big Anthony.

"Very good," said Mr. Ocean. "Every year on April 15th, grownups have to pay their taxes."

"That stinks!" said Annabelle.

"Yes it does!" said Mr. Ocean. "It is why I always get grumpy in April- I don't like having to send in a bunch of money."

The kids agreed that they wouldn't like to, either.

When school ended, Mr. Ocean handed out a sealed envelope to every kid as they left the room. "Make sure you give this to your parents," he explained. The kids promised to do just that.

❤   ❤   ❤

The next morning, Mrs. Stabler stormed into Mr. Ocean's room while the kids were in music class. "What were you thinking yesterday?" she yelled.

"Um, about what?" He said. The kids weren't sure if he was playing dumb, or if he had actually forgotten. With Mr. Ocean, it actually could've gone either way.

"When you sent a bill home to your students' parents!" She held up a copy of the bill, which one of the parents had given her. "You're trying to charge an extra $86 per child for 'educational expenses'?"

"Oh, that," he said, "Well, I thought it wasn't unreasonable. I'm quite a good teacher, after all, and I thought that the parents might not mind chipping in a little bit of extra money to cover the special attention that I provide."

"You already get paid by the school!" shouted Mrs. Stabler. You can't ask the parents for more money. What were you thinking?"

"Well, taxes are due in a few days," said Mr. Ocean. "I was hoping to collect some money so I could pay my taxes."

"Don't you have enough money for your taxes?"

"Well, of course I have it, I just don't really want to spend it. I like to think of my bank account as a one-way street: money comes in, but it never leaves."

Mrs. Stabler rolled her eyes. Mr. Ocean promised that it would never happen again.

"Have you forgotten you're on your second strike? This looks like it might just be your third!"

"Maybe I should remind you of something," suggested Mr. Ocean.

"What?" she demanded.

"Well, I know you've enjoyed taking credit for our very successful school garden. I've heard you telling lots of parents how you had the idea and just knew it would work out. Well, it sure would be a shame if they heard about who really had the idea in the first place."

"You wouldn't dare!"

"Maybe I would."

The two adults stared at each other in silence for a minute, neither one saying a word or giving in. Finally they came to a truce.

"Ok," said Mrs. Stabler. "Consider this to be just a warning. If any other parents say anything, I'll tell them that you are just a harmless, confused old man and you didn't really mean it. That it was your idea of a joke. I'll let this one go- but you'd better be on your best behavior: I'm watching you!"

With that, she stormed out.

"Whew," thought Mr. Ocean. "That could have been a lot worse. And the best part is that five parents actually gave their kids checks to give me this morning! That's $430 I didn't have before!"

WASATCH

ARTS

ACADEMY

Chapter Seventeen

Kids in every grade still talked about the famous "I'm with Stupid" incident that had occurred at the assembly on the first day of school- you don't easily forget something like that!- but on the first of May, Principal Stabler called everyone to the auditorium for an assembly that would be remembered for a very different reason: she was about to deliver some terrible news.

"I have some bad news, everybody," she began. The students quieted down instantly- everyone was curious about what it could be.

"It turns out," she continued, "That the school district doesn't have the money to continue the arts programs at Wasatch. That means no art, music, dance, or drama after this school year!"

This was a bombshell of the highest order. The students couldn't imagine worse news. Wasatch was lucky in that it focused heavily on the arts- kids from all over the city, in fact, were jealous.

"What can we do?" asked one of the fourth grade teachers.

"Well, the district has agreed that we can continue the programs if we can raise the money ourselves."

A cheer went up throughout the auditorium. Maybe things would be just fine after all!

"Hold on, hold on," urged Mrs. Stabler, "I am afraid that we have an impossible challenge ahead of us."

"How much do we need?" asked a fifth grade teacher.

"A lot. $25,000." She allowed this to sink in. The crowd was fairly quiet, with a few murmured conversations here and there.

"Well, how much have we raised in our fundraisers in the past?" asked a first grade teacher.

"Not nearly enough. The most we've ever raised before was $9,000." Mrs. Stabler looked down, as if she was unable to meet the eyes of all of the students who were looking to her for a miracle.

Suddenly something crazy happened. Something totally unexpected. Something that was so weird that it just might work.

"Ahem," said Mr. Ocean as he stood up from his seat. "I have a suggestion to make."

All eyes were upon him: what could he possibly say next?

"A fundraiser like this seems like an impossible task. You're going to need someone to run it and make sure that we raise every nickel we can. To make sure that we don't waste a penny along the way."

"That's funny," said a sixth grade teacher who had never been particularly fond of Mr. Ocean. "You sure know a thing or two about not wasting any pennies!"

Laughter erupted around the auditorium. Mr. Ocean's cheapness, of course, was legendary, and no one could deny that he often got a little bit "creative" when it came to making and saving money.

"You're right," agreed Mr. Ocean. "And that is why I am volunteering to run the fundraiser. It is no secret around here that making extra money is one of my hobbies, after all."

Mr. Ocean's students cheered. What a feeling of pride to think that their weird old teacher was actually trying to do the right thing for once! That he might actually save the arts at Wasatch!

Mrs. Stabler looked shocked. She was, in fact, speechless for a minute or so. "Well," she stammered, "I guess that's true, you actually are pretty good at making money. But this is going to take a lot of work- why are you so interested in helping?"

"For the children," he said solemnly, "For the children."

With that, the students all across the auditorium leapt to their feet and began clapping and hooting.

"I guess that makes it official," thought Mrs Stabler. "I just hope he can make this work. And I still don't know if I trust his reasons. 'For the children'? That doesn't sound like him at all."

Mrs. Stabler was right to be suspicious: Mr. Ocean did in fact have a reason for volunteering that he was keeping to himself. If he let his secret slip out, the consequences could be huge. Anyway, he *was* doing the right thing, but not for the reason he claimed.

Meet Mr. Ocean

Chapter Eighteen

The next day after school, a group of parents and teachers got together as a committee to discuss the fundraiser.

"First we need to come up with some fundraiser ideas," said Mr. Ocean. "And somebody should write them up on the board."

Everybody looked at him curiously. "What? Why don't you just do it?"

"Writing on the board tires me out," he explained. The parents and teachers rolled their eyes and shook their heads, but they moved on and soon enough they began coming up with ideas. Unfortunately, their thinking wasn't all that creative.

"The problem," said Mr. Ocean, "is that these ideas are just your normal, average kind of ideas. Sell magazine? Sell cookies? Sure, those are ok, but we've done them a million times, and they don't even raise that much money. We need to think outside of the box."

Everybody was silent. "Ok," sighed Mr. Ocean, "Here's what I'm thinking. We are a pretty unusual school."

"Yeah, because you work here!" said one of the fathers. Mr. Ocean ignored the comment, partially because it was true and he couldn't argue with it.

"What I mean is that we are the only arts school in the city, and that makes us pretty special. All of our kids gets to take a ton of music, art, dance, and drama classes. I think we should figure out a way to use that unique advantage to raise money."

Nobody said anything. "Ok," said Mr. Ocean, "Here's an idea. Write this down. How about every child makes a piece of artwork and we put them all in the gym and have a huge art show? We have 500 kids in this school, so I think this is a big opportunity."

The parents and teacher sat up a little straighter in their seats and began to talk quietly. They seemed to like the idea.

"And what's more," continued Mr. Ocean, "We can have it advertised on tv. I don't know if anybody will remember this, but back in September, the tv news showed the assembly that presented Mrs. Stapler as our new principal, and we could just give them a call- I'm sure they'd do a story about us."

"Wow!" said one of the teachers, "This could make

us a fortune! If we charged between $5 and $20 for each piece of art, it could make us a few thousand dollars in just a day!"

Mr. Ocean smiled. "And that is just one of my ideas. Ready for some more?"

Everybody smiled and nodded. Mr. Ocean continued.

"Most of you probably realize that we have a great ballet company, and that they perform pretty often with music played by the Utah Symphony. Well, I think we should approach them with an unusual offer: we could come up with a special dance routine that could be performed with them, and our kids who play instruments could play with the symphony. We could split the profits with the ballet and symphony and it would probably be a real hit."

"Yes!" exclaimed the same father who had questioned Mr. Ocean just moments before.

"And then, how about we have the kids write a play and perform it? If we start soon, we could have enough time for it."

The parents and teachers of the fundraiser committee jumped up and began to clap.

"Perfect!" they shouted. "Incredible!"

The rest of the meeting was spent planning how to make it all happen. They decided to meet three times per week until the end of school to keep everything on track. It would be a lot of work, but it looked possible.

• • •

The next day in Mr. Ocean's class, Chuck the squirrel was hanging out with the kids, running from desk to desk, looking for any extra food that he could find.

"Mr. Ocean!" exclaimed Annabelle. "I've got an idea! I was just thinking about how popular Chuck is with the kids in our class, and I thought, I bet the kids in the rest of the school would love him too!"

"True," agreed Mr. Ocean, not sure where this was going.

"So what about this: we give every kid in school the chance to get his picture taken with Chuck. If we charged a dollar, we could collect $500!"

Mr. Ocean considered this. "Great idea!" he said after a minute. "But I think we could charge a little more. After all, this is a really unusual opportunity. Let's ask for five dollars instead."

The kids agreed. It was definitely a lot more money, but they agreed that it was probably a once-in-a-lifetime opportunity.

"And one more thing," said Mr. Ocean, "If people start asking questions about Chuck, and why he's so tame, and so comfortable in our classroom, we just have to act as if we don't know why. They probably won't believe us, but they won't be able to prove that he's actually our class pet."

The kids and nodded in agreement. They decided to advertise by word of mouth so that they didn't have anything written down that might get Mr. Ocean or themselves into trouble. They told a few kids in a few other classes, and from there on, the word got around- if you want your picture taken with a real, live squirrel, just show up at Mr. Ocean's room. The plan worked perfectly, and they made a ton of money.

Chris Gleason

Chapter Nineteen

The next month was super busy. Everyone worked incredibly hard on the art projects, dance practices, and everything else they'd need to do as part of Mr. Ocean's grand plan. The various fundraisers went on and were deemed a success. Local tv stations and newspapers pitched in to help, as Mr. Ocean had hoped, and this helped to attract a ton of attention to the school's plight- and to its plans to overcome the obstacles. Never before had the school managed to raise so much money in such a short time.

One day in early June, the kids found themselves with a bit of a quiet moment- most of the fundraiser activities were over with, and they wanted to make sure that they used every possible opportunity to raise the money they needed. Mr. Ocean's students were trying to come up with ideas as he walked in that morning.

"I was thinking that maybe we could sell tickets and raffle off a prize. Something really exciting!" suggested Mabel.

"Well, we already let kids get their picture taken with a squirrel," said Big Anthony, who couldn't imagine a more exciting prize than that.

"True, but there's got to be something else," said Joanna.

The kids hemmed and hawed, trying to think up a good prize- and it had to be something that they could realistically get their hands on and deliver. That turned out to be the hard part, of course.

"Well," said Tommy, "If we can't think of something good to raffle off, how about a good old fashioned car wash?"

 He explained that, as he walked to school that morning, he noticed a man washing their car in his driveway.

"That looks like fun!" Israel had said.

"Ugh, I wish!" groaned the man. "I can't stand having to do this. It is a real pain, but it costs too much to take it to the carwash. They're charging $15 these days!"

Well, thought Israel as he continued his walk, it sure looks like fun to me. And I'd do it for less than that!

"We could charge, like, five dollars," Tommy continued, "And people would love it because they'd be saving a fortune!"

Mr. Ocean mulled it over. "I like it," he said, "But let's charge ten dollars. I think people will still pay it because it is still a good savings for them compared to the carwash. We don't want to cut our prices too much, because then we won't make as much!"

The kids nodded in agreement. Plus getting to have a carwash sounded like a blast! They immediately started making posters to advertise for it, plus flyers to put on the windshields of all the cars they might walk by on the way to school. Mr. Ocean consulted the calendar and chose Saturday June 10th as the date. Excitement levels were high.

♥ ♥ ♥

The timing of the carwash ended up perfect. It had rained for two days before, which meant that every car in town was covered in dirt from driving through so many mud puddles. And the day of the carwash was bright and sunny and warm, which inspired a lot of people to want to get their messy cars cleaned up. So, it looked as though business might be booming. And it was.

Although it wasn't very well organized, the fact

that dozens of kids showed up- from kindergarten right on up through sixth grade- helped things to go just fine. They weren't particularly systematic in their approach, but every time a car pulled up in front of the school, at least ten or twelve kids jumped up to begin scrubbing it down. Nobody cared who did what- by the time they were through, every car was just immaculate. The car owners were only too pleased to hand Mr. Ocean their ten dollars- a few even handed over a little extra as a tip for the fine service they'd gotten.

Near the end of the day, with the sun high in the sky, the temperature was really getting up there. Most of the kids were soaking wet from hosing down cars all day, but Mr. Ocean had managed to stay pretty dry. However, he was getting way too hot.

"That's it!" he declared, "I'm roasting!" and with that, he pulled his shirt off and flipped his beard over his shoulder. "Ahhhh," he said, "Much better!"

At exactly that time, a grey station wagon pulled in, and a familiar face leaned out the open window. It was Mrs. Stabler.

"We're not going to charge you, Mrs. Stapler," said Tommy Tibbler, "You're our principal and you work hard enough."

"Thank you, Tommy, that's very sweet. In that case, I would like to make a small donation, but there is one catch."

The kids gathered around, curious about what she'd say next.

"I'll give you ten dollars, but only if Mr. Ocean puts his shirt back on. That is a sight I never want to see again. And he has to keep it on for the rest of the carwash- I'm afraid he'll scare away the customers!"

"Well, I am feeling a lot more comfortable this way," said Mr. Ocean with a small smile, "But I'd like us to get that ten dollars, so I guess I can put my shirt back on."

The kids cheered wildly- for both Mrs. Stabler and Mr. Ocean.

Chapter Twenty

Mr. Ocean stood up and began to announce how much money each of the various fundraisers had raised.

"As you all know, we had a number of different fundraisers. I will tell you how much they each raised, and Mrs. Stabler will write the numbers down on the chalkboard behind me. First of all, the carwash, which many of you helped at, raised $1240."

"The art sale," he said, was huge. It raised $7,100!"

"Remember the joint performance where we teamed up with the Salt Lake Ballet Company and the Utah Symphony? This was our biggest success. We raised $9000!"

"As for the play that you all wrote and performed… well, that made $2076."

"In addition," he continued, "One of the classes provided the opportunity to have your picture taken with a squirrel, and that raised $1395."

Mrs. Stabler added up the numbers. " But we're still short of our goal!" she yelled in a panic.

"Well," said Mr. Ocean with a twinkle in his eye,

"We're not quite done yet. I'm sure you all remember the spring concert?"

Heads nodded all over the auditorium. "Well, I decided to record it, just to remember it by. Once I'd listened to it a few times, I realized how good it was. I decided to have it made into a CD, and I sold it on the internet. I am donating 100% of the profits to the fundraiser!"

Cheers broke out across the room. "How much did it make?" asked Mrs. Stabler breathlessly.

"$2250," he announced.

Mrs. Stabler- and everybody else in the crowd, except the kindergarteners who weren't capable- did the math. "That's still not enough!" shouted the principal.

"As it turns out," said Mr. Ocean, "There's more. The kids in my class might remember the drawing contest that they entered at Thanksgiving." Of course they did, and they nodded their heads accordingly.

"Well," he said, "I was so impressed by the quality of the drawings- not just from the winners, but from everybody in the class- that I had them made into posters, which I also sold online. If you kids don't mind, I suggest that we donate all of the profits to the fundraiser!"

"Yes!" they cried. "How much did we raise?"

"$785!"

Mrs. Stabler looked grim. "I hate to say it," she said, "But we're still short. You can't possibly have one more thing to contribute, do you?"

"As a matter of fact, I do. And this should really surprise you. At Christmas time, my students gave me a beautiful watch. I could tell it was a fine antique, and as soon as I received it back in December, I showed it to an expert, who told me its true value. I kept it, because I liked owning something that was worth a lot of money, but just a few days ago, I decided that there was something better than having an expensive watch."

"So I sold it, he said, "And I'm donating the money to the fundraiser. Anybody want to guess how much it was worth?"

The crowd was silent. Nobody dared guess- plus they really had no idea. "I sold it for $1,470," he said."

Everyone thought about it for a minute. Mrs.

Stabler jumped up. "$25,316. That means we met our goal!" she hollered!

And then something happened that no one would've ever dared to imagine: Mrs. Stabler ran to Mr. Ocean and gave him a huge hug. You could tell he was shocked: but then, so was everybody else.

Everyone in the room jumped to their feet and began to clapping.

"We saved the arts!" shouted Mrs. Stabler, letting go of Mr. Ocean. "We saved the arts!"

The hooting, hollering, and cheering seemed like it would never end.

♥   ♥   ♥

Everybody wanted to hug Mr. Ocean, shake his hand, and whisper words of thanks into his ear. He seemed a bit embarrassed by it all, but he accepted his moment of fame well enough. "Head back to the room, kids," he told his students, "I'll be right there."

When the kids arrived, they noticed something unprecedented. The door to his Secret Closet of Doom was slightly ajar.

"Do you think we should look inside?" asked Suzie timidly.

"No!" said Big Anthony. "I'm too young to die!"

"Oh come on," said Israel, "There can't be anything

dangerous in there. Mr. Ocean was just trying to scare us to keep us away."

"Which means that there must be something really good inside," said Annabelle.

When they looked in, they couldn't believe their eyes.

For one thing, it was huge.

"That's not a closet!" said Mabel. "It's like a living room!"

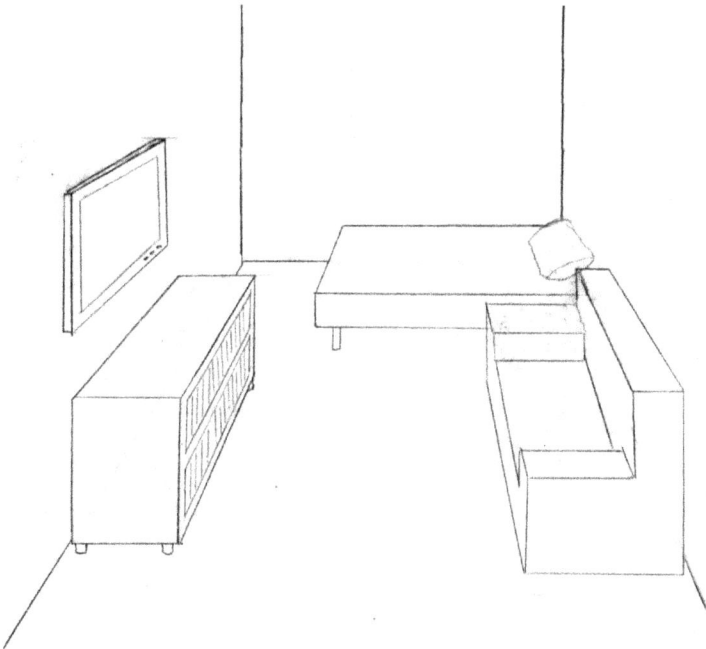

"Yeah, and it looks like a bedroom too!" said Tommy.

"Well, Mr. Ocean does like to be comfortable," said Joanna. "That would explain the bed AND the couch."

The closet was like no closet that they'd ever seen before. In addition to the bed and couch, it contained a dvd player and a whole bookshelf full of dvd's.

"Do you think he lives here?" asked Mabel.

"Nah, I think he has a regular house," said Israel. "I think he's talked about it a couple of times."

"Wait a minute," yelled Annabelle suddenly. "Is that our old smartboard? It is! He must've figured out a way to make it work like a tv!"

Just then, Mr. Ocean walked in.

"Mr. Ocean!" uttered Big Anthony, "You could get in big trouble if Mrs. Stapler saw this!"

Mr. Ocean froze like a deer in headlights. The kids whispered about what to do. "Don't worry," said Israel, "We're not going to tell. You saved the arts! Who cares if you have a closet with a bed in it." With that, they made their way to their seats.

Mr. Ocean went through a range of emotions. He

walked into the room full of pride, then a wave of panic almost knocked him over. When the found out the kids would keep his secret, a sense of profound relief washed over him.

"Ok kids," he announced. "Let's go outside for an extra-long recess!"

Out near the swings, Mabel walked up to her teacher. "Mr. Ocean?" she asked. "Would you like me to push you on the swing?"

He thought about it for a minute. "No, Mabel. Let me push you. That's what a good teacher would do." She hopped on the swing and Mr. Ocean did his best impression of a quality educator.

"You are a good teacher, Mr. Ocean," said Mabel, "You're just a weird dude. I mean, yes, you're lazy, cheap, and forgetful, but you manage to take care of the important things. And sometimes, you really go above and beyond."

Mr. Ocean didn't know what to say. "Mabel, I have gotten a lot of compliments today," he said, "And that's something I'm not very used to. But yours definitely means the most."

Over by the slides, Annabelle talked with one of the first graders. "What if I have him next year?"

she asked. "I used to hear that he was the worst teacher in the world, but after the fundraiser, that can't really be true, can it?

"Well, I've had a whole schoolyear to get to know him," said Annabelle. "And no, he is not the worst teacher in the world. Sure, he is kind of a pain in the neck a lot of the time, but he was ok at teaching, and I guess he did a lot of funny stuff along the way. I wouldn't call him the 'worst' teacher in the world. I guess I'd have to call him 'the weirdest teacher in the world' instead."

As Mr. Ocean watched the kids run around the playground, he reflected on how well things had worked out. For everybody, really.

"I'm just glad they didn't ask any more questions about my closet," he said. "I don't think I could've lied to those kids. But I definitely didn't want to tell the truth, either- I like having a secret hideaway where I can relax and watch some tv while they're off at their arts classes. I mean, if they didn't have music, dance, art, and drama to go to, I'd have to do a lot more teaching!"

He shuddered at the thought of what had almost come to pass. It had been a lot of hard work over the past month, making sure the fundraiser was a success, but for Mr. Ocean, it was worth it. He wouldn't have to make any changes in his lazy teaching style, and if he'd ended up looking like a hero, that was a pretty good bonus. At least it might help keep Mrs. Stabler off his back for a while.

The End

ABOUT THE AUTHOR

Chris Gleason is a professional woodworker who lives in Salt Lake City with his wife Michele and daughter Abigail. He has written eleven books for the DIY woodworking market, and is well known for his expertise in designing and building with reclaimed woods. This is his first work of fiction that is polished enough to release into the wild.

Meet Mr. Ocean